Easy Tarot
Handbook

About the Author

For Josephine Ellershaw, the Tarot has been a constant life companion on a personal journey that now spans more than three decades. Professionally, she has many years of experience providing readings, healing, and metaphysical guidance to an international clientele.

She lives in North Yorkshire, England, with her family and a large menagerie of pets, including waifs, strays, and rescues.

Please visit her website at www.learn-tarot-cards.com.

To Write to the Author

If you wish to contact the author or would like more information about this book, please write to the author in care of Llewellyn Worldwide and we will forward your request. Both the author and publisher appreciate hearing from you and learning of your enjoyment of this book and how it has helped you. Llewellyn Worldwide cannot guarantee that every letter written to the author can be answered, but all will be forwarded. Please write to:

Josephine Ellershaw
% Llewellyn Worldwide
2143 Wooddale Drive, Dept. 978-0-7387-1150-8
Woodbury, MN 55125-2989, U.S.A.

Please enclose a self-addressed stamped envelope for reply,
or $1.00 to cover costs. If outside the U.S.A., enclose
an international postal reply coupon.

Many of Llewellyn's authors have websites with additional information and resources. For more information, please visit our website at http://www.llewellyn.com.

EASY TAROT
HANDBOOK

Josephine Ellershaw

Illustrations from the Gilded Tarot Deck

by Ciro Marchetti

First Edition
Seventh Printing, 2009

Edited by Lee Lewis Walsh
Cover art © Ciro Marchetti
Cover design by Gavin Dayton Duffy
Llewellyn is a registered trademark of Llewellyn Worldwide, Ltd.

ISBN-13: 978-0-7387-1150-8
ISBN-10: 0-7387-1150-0

Llewellyn Publications
A Division of Llewellyn Worldwide, Ltd.
2143 Wooddale Drive, Dept. 978-0-7387-1150-8
Woodbury, Minnesota 55125-2989, U.S.A.
www.llewellyn.com

Printed in the United States of America

Dedication

In loving memory of my father, John,
who taught me the power of belief.

Acknowledgments

To those I love, whose presence inspires the colours of my life . . .

There are a number of people to whom I wish to extend my sincere thanks for their support and encouragement—had it not been so, then this book would never have been written.

My family were incredibly understanding during the process of writing the book, which was written for the most part while they slept: Daphne, who rallied round to always "keep the home fires burning"; everyone should have a mum like mine. Robert and Emily, my children, who took it all in stride, with encouragement and sense of humour throughout.

My good friend Sheila, who periodically nipped next door to share cups of tea and dish out moral support, in the *very* early hours of the morning.

Reid, who reminded me that the pursuit of our dreams is founded upon passion.

Lisa Finander, my editor, for her enthusiasm and encouragement as she steered me through the entire process.

Last, but far from least, the amazing people from all over the globe, "met" through my website, who have touched my life with their experiences, personal challenges, and beautiful messages.

Thank you!

Contents

Part Two: Meeting the Tarot 33

Part Three: Preparation for Readings 139

Namaste.

The Tarot has remained my constant companion on a journey
that has now spanned more than
three decades, during which time
they have never failed to amaze
or bring comfort with their pro-
found system of wisdom and
guidance.

Over the years, I was intrigued
by the number of people who informed me they owned a Tarot
deck, but said it was unused "in a drawer somewhere" because
they hadn't been able to learn the cards.

It caused me to look back, to remember my own frustrations in learning Tarot, and finally I wrote *Easy Tarot* in the
hope that I could make readers' paths easier and prevent some
of the struggles that are sometimes encountered.

This book contains the exact format and information that
I use to conduct readings, and follows a step-by-step process of
learning I call "The Tarot Technique" that has worked for me
and the people I subsequently shared it with, so for the moment
I ask only that you follow the steps in the order provided.

When Llewellyn accepted this book, they asked if I could
break my method down into "steps." As I did so, and without
design, it naturally broke down into twenty-two steps, which
also corresponds to the number of cards in the major arcana. It
made me smile. Such are the endless wonders of Tarot, so I felt
inclined to share that little snippet with you.

I share this knowledge and experience with you in my sincere hope that the Tarot will enrich your life as it has mine, and I wish you every success along your path.

Enjoy the journey . . .
Josie

Foreword

A journey has often been used as a metaphor for the Tarot—the Fool's journey, or a personal journey to find meaning, clarification, or direction in one's own life or that of the querent. So within this context, how do we proceed along this journey? How do we read the signs along the way to better understand where we are and where our road leads?

There are seventy-eight standard images of the Tarot, divided into the major and minor arcanas, suits, and elements. What do they mean in general and, possibly even more relevant, what do they mean to us personally in a given reading?

To me, they seem like a map for our journey; each card with its specific number and title serves almost like a street sign. A useful start, certainly, but not in itself the complete answer. But by viewing the cards relative to other cards within a spread and within the context of questions being asked, the answers become clearer. To return to my analogy of the map, in addition to the street sign we now also know that we are facing east or west, or are at a corner or crossroads, thus providing us with a more specific reference. But there are richer levels still; the symbolism and visual content contained in the cards can offer so much more. On our imaginary street, we can observe shadows to provide us with a sense of what time of the day it is, while the temperature might provide an indication of the season. Observing the surrounding buildings and passersby, filtered through our own life experience, can provide clues as to whether we are in an affluent neighborhood or a poor one, dangerous or safe, and where we are along our journey.

So what role does the imagery of any given deck have in this process? Is one style better suited than another? Certainly in the hands of an experienced reader, there may be less need for the detail of a fully illustrated deck. Indeed, it might even prove a distraction, and deeper, more personal interpretations might be achieved via the plainer, less illustrated style of the Marseilles decks, for example. But when initially introduced to the world of Tarot, I was immediately drawn to the fully illustrated content of the traditional Rider-Waite deck, and the Gilded Tarot pays homage to that style and structure.

For the most part I've remained quite faithful to that form, and those already familiar with the Rider-Waite deck should feel quite comfortable in using the Gilded Tarot. For those who use the Gilded Tarot as their learning deck, they should also feel comfortable when they wish to expand and experience other decks.

Beyond being a set of symbol-filled images, most decks also serve as a vehicle for artistic expression, and provide ample opportunity for the deck's creator to include his or her personal interpretation and character while still keeping within the traditional Tarot structure.

Within the Gilded Tarot you will find many elements, such as machine parts or animals, which do not appear in the strictest Tarot tradition. They are personal touches that reflect my general illustrative style. If you wish, they can viewed as simple decorative backdrops—theatrical props, as it were, that may enrich the Tarot experience, but they also allow ample flexibility for you to add your own interpretations.

In the broader sense, the various mechanical devices have no specific function, but serve as symbols of mankind's involvement and interaction with the natural and spiritual order of things. Opportunities or events that come our way may be fate, but what we make of them varies based on our own response and intervention. We are not merely puppets at the whim of the gods.

The inclusion of animals in various cards is also a personal choice. Many creatures already have meanings and symbolism attached to them. The owl, for example, is associated with nighttime and wisdom, but its role in the Gilded Nine of Swords still provides opportunity for you to add your own personal associations. These interpretations don't need to remain static, either, but may well vary from one reading to another. In this way I hope the Gilded Tarot can serve as a user-friendly companion to those starting on their Tarot journey, but it also has the flexibility to remain a faithful companion as you become more traveled.

Being involved in the production of a Tarot deck has been a truly satisfying experience. I can't think of many other creative fields where so much attention is paid to one's work. Due to its role and function, the imagery of a Tarot card is scrutinized perhaps to a greater degree than any other visual medium. The interpretation an artist provides for any given card may not be universally embraced by everyone in the Tarot community, but it would appear that, for the most part, the Gilded Tarot has been well received. I have received numerous e-mails indicating that it had played a role in motivating someone to take up Tarot, either for the first time or when returning to it after some period of absence. As an artist, that is extremely satisfying.

Ciro Marchetti

Good Foundations

Part One

Just a few words before we begin on how to get the best from this book. I know it's very tempting to jump in, lay out some cards, and then check the meanings. Before you do, let me say—please don't!

Please restrain the urge to dive in and "have a go," as I learned this was one of the main reasons people became frustrated or overwhelmed and then failed to learn the cards. There needs to be a level of understanding, a foundation upon which to gradually build your knowledge; one needs to learn the tools of a trade before engaging them. If you were learning to be a surgeon, you wouldn't expect to perform surgery in your first lesson!

I'm sure you have heard this analogy: if you hold a magnifying glass in one place over a piece of paper in sunlight, it will, after a period of time, begin to scorch and burn. However, if you continuously move it around, then nothing will happen. Similarly, please use your concentrated effort to follow through the information in the order it's presented to you, as it has been designed to naturally follow for your development. By skipping back and forth you will miss some important connections.

If your curiosity can't be contained, then quickly read through the whole book—but once you start the learning process, follow the recommended format. To put your mind at ease, I'm not suggesting that you're going to be studying in the conventional sense, as if preparing for an examination. As we cover each card or area, you don't need to try to memorize everything before moving on to the next part. By using the suggested format of study, combined with the way Tarot works, once we have covered each card your subconscious will retain the information—whether you're aware of it or not!

It is a natural reaction to want to try a reading on yourself as you progress, so neither am I suggesting that you must go through every single card individually before doing this, just so long as in the meantime you continue with the given format. There is a reason for everything I suggest to you, and wherever possible I will provide examples to explain my reasoning.

When I first began, I did precisely what I'm asking you not to do! I dove into the book that accompanied my cards and tried self-readings, referring to the book for the card meanings. I was only twelve at the time and the book didn't actually provide any kind of advice for a learning process . . . so back and forth in the book I'd go. I literally wore the pages out! I must have been very determined, for it was a lengthy process. I learned the cards and performed readings but, some years later, everything changed quite dramatically for me once I developed the learning technique I'm sharing with you now. So you see, I'm not just dishing out a theory to you here, or something that seems like a good idea of how I think you should go about things.

You will require a certain amount of patience if you are serious in your quest, but the book is presented in a set, step-by-step format so it should flow more easily for you. Even if you have studied Tarot before, please read through the book in the order intended. I can only give you my assurance it will pay dividends in the longer term. Don't be discouraged. The Tarot always rewards diligence and sincerity of purpose.

What we can do at this stage, though, is look at some of the basics about the Tarot and the mixing pot of ingredients you should be aware of, before we look at the cards in depth.

STEP I

Background

It all starts with you . . .

I feel it is important for you to understand your own reasons for wanting to learn Tarot. You may not have really considered this before. Perhaps you just feel attracted to the cards sufficiently enough to want to learn more about them. That's fine, nothing wrong with that, but your reason is probably the main thing that will keep you going. Being able to receive personal guidance is quite a good reason—and I can honestly say, the Tarot has never let me down.

So if you can, identify your reason or reasons now—and write them down! Having a goal to aim for will help you achieve your objective, rather than aimlessly drifting along. It is your underlying reason that will encourage your perseverance.

Since this is a rather one-sided conversation, I shall assume that you are a complete beginner to the world of Tarot. So forgive me if you have traveled this road before, but this way I can ensure that nothing is left out or left unexplained, leaving you dangling in mid-air somewhere.

Perhaps your first introduction to the Tarot was through actually having a reading yourself, but in whatever way you came into contact with the cards, their mysterious images resonated somewhere deep within and beckoned you to follow.

No history lesson

There seems to be an endless supply of theories over the origin of Tarot cards, and most books usually include some version of their history. However, I won't go into detail about that here, as it is an issue of continuing debate.

The history of the Tarot appears to be as mysterious as the cards themselves, with many different cultures laying claim to some connection, along with varying theories and speculation as to how they evolved. I find it most apt that their universal appeal can be traced to so many cultures. No matter which civilization, continent, or timeline we examine, there appears to be a common thread; a theory that emerges throughout—that the Tarot was created using a secret code of symbols and images, to preserve the knowledge of a secret doctrine.

Factual history traced so far leads to fourteenth-century Italy, and while the Tarot in whatever form may have existed centuries before, there is considerable conjecture (but inconclusive evidence) to support these theories at the present time . . . perhaps it will always remain so. If you are interested, many books explore the history of the Tarot in depth.

Our concern here is in learning the cards in order to receive their guidance and, thankfully, knowledge of their history won't improve your ability to read Tarot cards any better. The most important fact is that they work! The rest of this book is laid out in such a way as to show you how they work and how to gain access to their knowledge.

About the Tarot deck

Firstly, let us consider the actual Tarot itself, how it is ordered, and what it consists of. The Gilded Tarot contains a total of seventy-eight cards, of which twenty-two are known as the major arcana, using Roman numerals 0–XXI. The remaining fifty-six are referred to as the minor arcana.

The minor arcana is then broken down into four different suits—wands, cups, swords, and pentacles. Each suit contains an ace through a ten, followed by a page, knight, queen, and king (known as court cards). Each of the suits represents one of the four elements:

Wands—Fire
Cups—Water
Swords—Air
Pentacles—Earth

The cards contain archetypal images, pictures, and symbols that make a connection with one's subconscious mind. The major arcana focuses on the higher matters of life, while the minor arcana indicates situations in our daily existence. But both are important. Think of the major arcana as the bricks and the minor as the mortar that fills the spaces, holding it all together.

Introducing the Gilded Tarot

Somehow I have the sneaking suspicion that you have already unwrapped your new Tarot cards to take a peek—and who could resist such a temptation?

I have purchased a great many cards over the years; in fact, my home is littered with unused Tarot decks. There is nothing more disappointing than thinking you have found *the* deck, only to discover that you can't work with it. There have been quite a number that have fit into that category for me—once laid out, the cards all appeared muted, with no solar plexus reaction, or the interpretations that I'm happy with just didn't fit with the images.

Like most people who love Tarot, I was constantly searching for the "perfect" working deck, like the search for the Holy Grail . . . and finally I found it in the Gilded Tarot, created by Ciro Marchetti and published by Llewellyn. Now I use nothing else. I believe they are the most visually stunning Tarot cards available and they immediately became the favorite deck for many in the Tarot community, readers and collectors alike.

The Gilded Tarot is breathtakingly beautiful; the magic and mystery of its images instantly transport you into another dimension. This is really most important, for your cards should provoke an instant inner response, regardless of whether you understand it. With each image presented, it is akin to becoming immersed in the scene and merging into the story. How I wish these cards had been available when I first began to learn!

Most people learn with what is termed "a beginner's deck," and then transfer to one they prefer later. There is a huge number of Tarot decks available, but many of the images and interpretations vary, so if you do change it can be like learning all over again. By using the Gilded Tarot, you will be saved from major frustrations from the beginning and if you don't feel the need to transfer to something else afterward, you get the best of both worlds—a double whammy!

STEP 2

Answering Your Questions

How does Tarot work?

Each of the seventy-eight cards contains a message within its image, a secret to share with you, designed to provide the necessary guidance required at that particular time, to help you in your quest upon the road called life.

The cards' message is communicated by the way they are prepared and chosen—their positioning once laid out in a "spread," and also by their relationship or association with one another based on proximity.

The Tarot is like a secret map we can consult along our journey, so that we can recognize the opportunities or pitfalls that may arise on our path.

The Tarot contains images that help the reader access information. They act as stepping stones among the conscious, subconscious, and super-conscious. The depth and accuracy of the reading depends upon the sensitivity of the person reading the cards. I have never found the Tarot to be "wrong," only misinterpreted.

Some say the Tarot acts as a mirror of ourselves, and while I agree with this, I would also venture further. I can only speak from personal experience, but the Tarot has frequently revealed situations and information that neither the reader nor the questioner knew about prior to the reading, but were found to be accurate upon further investigation. The cards have an uncanny accuracy and therefore make an excellent personal guidance system.

The Tarot can be used as a tool for personal guidance, for divining the future, to obtain universal wisdom, and for personal development, spiritual growth, and meditation.

Who uses Tarot cards?

The Tarot is non-denominational, so its appeal is universal. People from all different cultures, age groups, and walks of life consult the Tarot; the reality of this has become even more apparent for me since I launched my website. The Internet has made the world a smaller place! With thousands of users, my website provides a wider and more intriguing picture as I hear from so many different types of people.

Age-wise, people from teenagers to grandparents are represented. Occupationally, there are businesspeople, consultants, doctors, teachers, artists, therapists, counselors, factory workers, office workers, executives . . . the list goes on. People from all around the globe use Tarot; most countries are represented, as are many different belief systems and religious backgrounds.

Do I need to be psychic?

You don't need a special gift to read Tarot. However, what you will discover is that the more you work with the Tarot and these studies, the more your intuition will heighten and your psychic ability increase.

Everyone naturally has some degree of intuition; it's just that they tend not to recognize it or listen to it. Psychic development is like a muscle: the more you exercise it, the more toned it becomes! There is a technique I will share with you that allows you to recognize this process, and we'll get to that in just a moment.

How soon will I be able to do readings?

Like any skill, reading the Tarot can be learned through practice, patience, and perseverance, and everyone learns at a different pace. This book is not designed as a "quick-fix, instant reader guide." The intention is to show you how to learn the cards thoroughly, the first time round. Once you become familiar and comfortable with the cards and a few spreads, you will be able to read for yourself in a relatively short period of time.

Some people recommend practicing on family and friends, but I strongly advise against this in the early stages. For the moment, and the way these studies are designed, we will concentrate on self-readings, until you have sufficient knowledge, confidence, and ability—before letting your new-found skills loose on others. Having said this, it seems only fair that I should explain my reasoning.

I cannot tell you how many times I have been contacted by worried people, often as a result of a reading done by someone who was inexperienced or irresponsible with the Tarot cards. It is said that a little knowledge is dangerous, and in this case I certainly agree. With knowledge comes power and it must be used wisely. The Tarot should be approached with sincerity and seriousness of purpose; treated with respect and reverence, never with frivolity or as a game. There are ethics involved and quite a responsibility should you decide to read for others.

For the moment, the only person you will practice on is yourself. If you are going to make some mistakes, then it is far better that you see and understand them, rather than inflicting wrong information upon others. And I'm sure you're already thinking, "But Josie, you don't know my friends, they're different . . ." Please trust me on this; I want to see you succeed, so I'm not going to give you bad advice. No matter how understanding or helpful your friends or family are— please don't practice on them when you're just starting. There comes a point when you can read for them if you wish, but I'll show you how to tell when you're ready—then it's entirely up to you.

Later, as a Tarot consultant, you will see for yourself that your words carry great weight. You will be surprised when you hear someone recount your reading, especially what was retained and what wasn't. On occasion, you will hear your words misinterpreted and misquoted—and that's when you know what you're doing! Imagine how it goes when you're just beginning.

Your friends mean well and I'm sure they would be more than happy for you to practice readings on them, but what happens when you only have half the story, or the wrong one? If you don't have the answers for things that appear in the reading, then it could weigh on their minds and worry them. How would that affect your confidence, and theirs in you? The people closest to us are often prone to lightheartedly jest with us, and sometimes in front of others—they mean no harm, but this can damage your confidence and, in the longer term, could affect others' ability to take you seriously.

I hope you are convinced enough to follow my advice, since irresponsible readers cause unnecessary upset to others— they also give the Tarot and ethical readers a bad name. I assure you that it will all pay off a bit further along in your journey.

Fate or free will?

Forewarned is forearmed—the Tarot gives excellent guidance but it is not your master. Everyone has choices throughout his or her lifetime, and we all accrue karma, good and bad, by our actions and choices.

The most powerful tool people have is the power of their thoughts, which can elevate or destroy them, depending upon their attitudes and their beliefs. Never underestimate the power of belief.

Many people consult the Tarot when faced with difficult decisions or situations. They may feel confused by events in their life or feel they have lost direction and can no longer see ahead clearly. Imagine how suggestible someone in this state of mind could be. So when you start reading for others, you need to treat their readings with sensitivity because your words will carry more weight than you realize.

Your role, through what you see, is to help unravel what is happening around them, and to help them to make sense of matters. You provide guidance, so they can make better-informed decisions and proceed with more confidence.

When you lay out someone's cards, it's like glimpsing through windows into his or her life.

The reading will reflect what may happen if clients proceed upon their existing path, depending to a certain extent upon how far in motion events already are. The problem is, if you plant a negative thought, it sticks in the client's mind and settles in her subconscious. This would then be extremely hard to work against. It's like saying, "Don't think of an elephant"—see what I mean?

People have enough challenges working against their own thought patterns and, for this reason, a great deal of what you see will happen as shown, because people find it extremely difficult to master their mind control. Their thoughts and their attitudes have brought them to their present position. This said, I have a number of clients who have successfully steered themselves through difficult situations by following the guidance of the cards, thus avoiding an outcome they didn't want.

It's useful to remember the following:

- Forewarned is forearmed.
- Action shapes destiny.
- You are the master and not the slave.

Disposing of a few myths and misconceptions

I sometimes receive mail from people who are concerned because someone told them that the Tarot is evil or dangerous, and somewhere along the line you may encounter the same. As is often the case, such statements are made due to misinformation or ignorance. The Tarot is a tool and, just as with anything, can be used for good or bad—this depends upon how the cards are used, what they are used for, and the person using them. Hence we come back to the importance of responsible practice.

Some people will ask about the cards because they are interested and want to understand, but others may have a strong opinion they wish to inflict upon you. Should you encounter the latter with this type of attitude, please don't feel the necessity to defend your position, or feel that it's your responsibility to educate them. There are those who are open-minded and those who are not.

About other ancient sciences

If you wished to "study" Tarot, you could spend a lifetime doing so, as there is so much information covering virtually every aspect of the cards. This said, there is no guarantee that such study will make you an excellent Tarot reader.

I'm sure some people will immediately disagree with me for saying that you don't need to understand the links between Tarot and astrology, numerology, alchemy, or kabbalah to produce good readings, but I believe this. Each of the ancient sciences requires considerable study to fully appreciate and understand it. I have always felt that the Tarot stands strongly enough in its own right, which is good news for you because it means you don't have to learn these other disciplines in order to interpret the cards and produce good readings!

If you want to look into any of these areas more deeply later, then by all means do so. Unless it really is your area of expertise, don't feel the need to introduce it into your reading. Some lengthen their readings by adding snippets from the other sciences; perhaps they feel it gives added value. But invariably, this information is of a very basic nature. The phrase "jack-of-all-trades but master of none" springs to mind, and if you learn Tarot well, there is no need to do this. As an example, I once went to a well-known consultant, but it ruined her credibility for me when she ventured into areas that clearly weren't her forte, which soon became evident. She was embarrassed, the reading ended soon after, and I never went back.

When the time comes and you have someone sitting in front of you for a reading, the bottom line is this—they don't care how much technical knowledge you may have. They don't want to be blinded by science and your amazing knowledge (however great it may be). What they want is an accurate reading . . . end of story. So unless your knowledge of other disciplines significantly contributes to this and you can explain it in language they will understand, I would leave it well alone.

STEP 3

Making Preparations

Caring for your Tarot cards

If you were given a precious gift of an ancient text preserved through time that held invaluable ageless wisdom, how would you care for it? I suspect you would take very good care of it indeed.

As you will discover, the relationship you share with your Tarot cards is very personal, so you will want to care for them accordingly. From the moment you start working with your cards, you begin developing a link with them, and they become infused with your personal energy. So it makes good sense to protect them from any outside influence that could upset this balance.

I treat my Tarot with the great respect I believe they deserve. Since I also do consultations for others, I have a number of decks in use at any given time—those for my studies, those I consult for my own guidance, and those I use for others. Some are kept in a pouch and some are wrapped in a cloth and then stored in a wooden container, with a separate cloth to lay them on to read them. I never put them down on a table, always on a cloth used only for this purpose, and I always put them back into their containers when I'm not using them. This may all sound a little extreme, but the cards are very sensitive to outside energy and vibrations.

A good starting point is to use a drawstring pouch to hold your cards and a cloth of around twenty-four inches square to lay them onto. Many people prefer cloth of a natural fiber, although I have used man-made textiles with equally good effect. A plain black reading cloth is preferable, since it provides an excellent backdrop without creating any visual distractions from the images on your cards.

Guidance and protection

Although initially you will use your cards to study them, it's still a good idea to start as you mean to go on. So whenever you remove the cards from their container, open with a brief request for guidance. You don't need to go through long, involved rituals for this to be effective.

You can phrase this request however you wish, even something simple such as, "I ask and give thanks to the universe for guidance, protection, and assistance." I say mine quietly in my mind, as I feel it is a private matter. Doing so creates a connection to your subconscious. It shows respect for your work and the information you are about to receive, and it helps to keep the energy of your working space free from negative vibrations. As you become more sensitive, you will notice how different people bring different atmospheres and energies. When you open yourself up for a reading, your aura (personal energy field) joins with the person for whom you are reading, so it is important to protect yourself.

I'm sure at some time you have been in the company of someone who was feeling really down, and once he or she left, you felt drained and slightly down yourself. I won't get into the mechanics of what happens to your energy field—but suffice it to say, you don't want to be left with someone else's confusion or feelings of emotional upheaval. For this purpose, using a quartz crystal with your Tarot works extremely well.

Using a crystal

It is not necessary for you to use a crystal if you prefer not to, but I feel it makes a difference. It provides an excellent way to protect yourself and your Tarot from surrounding energies. Straight from Mother Earth herself, natural quartz crystal is a wonderful amplifier of energy and can be programmed to store a thoughtform.

For this purpose you will need a small natural quartz crystal; it can be rough or polished and can be purchased from a mind, body, and spirit shop or on the Internet. If you are able to choose it in person, then pick the one that you seem particularly drawn to, or one that feels right for you when you hold it in your hand, as crystals emanate an energy field of their own. When you first obtain your crystal, you will want to cleanse it of any negative energy it may have collected on its long journey before it reached you. There are a number of ways to do this.

If you already use crystals then you can place the new one on a large cluster bed for twenty-four hours, but I will assume this not to be the case and will cover it from a beginner's viewpoint.

Choose one of the following cleansing methods:

- Hold the crystal under running water from a natural stream or the sea or

- Soak the crystal in water with sea salt (failing this, ordinary salt will do) for up to twenty-four hours, and then rinse with mineral water.

Then:

- Place your crystal on a window ledge where it can receive natural sunlight or moonlight for a full day or evening.

To dedicate and program your crystal:

The simple statement I provide will be sufficient, but if you wish to formulate your own, please give it careful consideration and write it down before you begin—ensure there can be no misunderstanding in what you're asking for!

Hold the crystal in the palm of your hand and repeat:

"I ask and give thanks to the universe for guidance, protection, and assistance.

This crystal is dedicated to [your name] and my work with the Tarot. Please protect myself, my cards, and my reading environment from negative energy; help me to receive clear guidance and to assist those who consult me for readings.

For the highest good of all concerned. Thank you."

Store your crystal with your Tarot and repeat the cleansing, dedicating, and programming sequence a few times throughout the year, or as often as you feel necessary.

Preparing your Tarot deck

If you haven't done so already, before breaking the cellophane wrapper of your new deck, lay your cloth onto the table. New cards are very slippery and Tarot cards are slightly larger than ordinary playing cards, plus there are seventy-eight of them, so it will feel like quite a handful until you become accustomed to them.

Feel free to examine your beautiful new cards and enjoy the images—but before you start racing ahead to check out what they all mean, gently shuffle them, card over card. Absolutely no fancy or "poker" type shuffling.

As a child I read somewhere that the cards should be shuffled using the left hand (representing the subconscious) and, since I'm right-handed, it took me a while to master this, but now I can't do it any other way. However, it doesn't make any difference; do what you're comfortable with. At this stage it's important just to go slowly and carefully, however awkward it may feel. Otherwise you'll be endlessly picking stacks up off the floor as they fly out of your hands. (It happens to us all, honestly.) Notice how the cards feel.

Next take a large cotton handkerchief (or just a large square of natural material), lay your cards in the center, and tie the corners of the material together so your cards are secured. Place the bundle underneath your pillow and sleep over it that night. Don't be surprised if you find the Tarot images in your dreams.

I usually sleep on new cards twice, not always consecutively, which I find is enough. Leave the cards bundled safely until you have the time to sit with them again. Notice how different they feel when you shuffle them this time. From here it is a case of shuffling them on a regular basis until they start to feel right and fall into place. You will notice a distinct change in their energy and how they feel in your hands.

For the purpose of your studies, you don't need to have a fully-prepared deck as you would for a reading, since you will extract cards to study. But I do recommend sleeping on the cards and doing some regular shuffling because we want your deck to become infused with your energy and for you to start to feel connected to it.

STEP 4

Keys to Learning

Your number one learning tool

Keeping a Tarot diary is an invaluable tool, not only as you begin your journey with the Tarot, but also as you progress in knowledge and experience. Similar to keeping a personal diary in which you log events on a daily basis, it's always forward-looking and progressive. Keeping a Tarot diary and the way you record the information can make a radical difference in how much you retain. For this reason, I refer to it as your number one learning tool.

What kind to use?

My personal preference is to use an A4-size spiral-bound book, with lined or grid paper. These are particularly good as they're easier to write in and stay flat when you're working—it can be immensely frustrating if you're trying to record your readings and the pages keep flipping over! As you complete each book, you are left with a permanent record of your readings, which you can store in chronological order. They are very interesting to refer back to and that is actually part of their purpose.

Your book needn't be expensive; in fact, if it is, you will probably resist the urge to write in it or feel that your work must be magnificently presented! Your diary is very much a working tool and when the flow of thoughts hits you, you really don't want to be distracted by such matters. The most important thing is recording the information as your subconscious provides it to you—just so long as you can read it later, that's all that counts.

How to record information and why

As we examine each individual card, I recommend holding it (or touching the picture with your fingers), then writing down the meaning as you say it out loud. This is a renowned learning principle that vastly improves retention of information.

For instance:

- If you read the information alone, you will retain ten percent
- But if you see it and say the information out loud as you write it down, you will retain ninety percent.

Quite a big difference, isn't there? So although it may seem like a chore, it will save you a great deal of time in the long run—and if you're going to do this, then it's just as well to do it right the first time.

It is also important to personalize the cards based on your experiences, thus avoiding "parrot syndrome"—simply memorizing the cards. So if the memory of a particular event that has happened to you is triggered by one of the card's meanings, make a note of this. In addition, you may find that experiences of people you know remind you of the cards' meanings, so make a note of that too. All of this helps the cards feel more personal and real to you—they start to represent real situations instead of just words in a book.

I will cover how to record readings once we get there, but here is an example of how to lay out your diary as you study each card:

Date:

0 The Fool	Card Meaning: • You may wish to use bullet points for this section Personal Experiences: • List any personal experiences that relate to this card's meaning Others' Experiences: • List others' experiences that remind you of this card

About dreams and psychic development

In addition to the conscious and subconscious, there is also a further element, which is sometimes referred to as the super-conscious, the universal consciousness, or the universal mind. Think of this as a pure stream of energy; it is the link between us all, the field of interconnectivity. This is where inspiration, inventions, ideas, and creativity manifest. More recently the term "cosmic ordering" has become fashionable (which concerns manifesting desires into reality), but it all comes down to the interaction between the three levels of consciousness.

The super-conscious is accessed via the subconscious, so you may discover that as your subconscious awakens to the subtleties around you, your awareness becomes more heightened. Dreams will seem more vivid and information may start filtering through, for when we are asleep the subconscious can express itself more readily, without our conscious thoughts interfering. In other words, we step out of our own way, allowing our intuition to flow freely.

As this begins to happen, also record in your diary anything that seems relevant from your dreams. Don't worry about the accuracy of your thoughts or information; no one is judging your results—except we are usually our own harshest critics. Sometimes the images you see or the words you hear are quite literal and straightforward; at other times they will be symbolic, or very personal in meaning.

For instance, sometimes I hear my mother call my name as if interrupting my dream, like a dream within a dream, and in a tone that I have learned to recognize as being warned about something around me. The significant part of this is that it is never connected to my dream, and it is so real it has woken me at times. One could argue that this may be telepathic, or just symbolic—either way, the motherly warning tone is significant to me and has become very accurate.

As with the Tarot, many of the images in dreams are symbolic, but by recording the dreams that stand out to you, you learn to communicate with your subconscious mind, learning a language that is personal to you and opening the lines of communication. For some it can be like opening a floodgate, but don't be alarmed by this; it is simply that your awareness has become heightened.

By recording this information, you will learn to decipher which are "normal" dreams and which are prophetic, for they feel very different. Many mornings I have awoken just "knowing" something, yet couldn't remember dreaming it. Don't be afraid to write such incidents down, for it is only in so doing that you learn from them. Resist the temptation to rush out and buy a dream dictionary—for it is your own intuition we are looking for, not another's interpretation of what "should" be.

Equally importantly, don't go into "overzealous mode," assuming that everything you dream is forewarning you of something. As with everything, moderation is the key.

Your intuition

Gradually, as you progress with your studies, you may discover that these same types of "dreams" transfer into your waking hours too, usually when you're doing something mundane, like washing dishes, and when you're not really concentrating on anything in particular. This happens when you have accessed the super-conscious and information easily transfers through. It is often referred to as intuition.

Record these moments too, for it is only in analyzing this information that you will understand the messages you are being given. This translates differently for each person and is very much an individual experience. Just to provide a few examples: you may experience "flash thoughts," with a certain feeling of knowingness, or you may "see" images, similar to daydreams. You may sense things when you are in people's company, or from an environment—this is usually felt in the solar plexus area and can feel like knots or butterflies in your stomach. You may smell things that aren't there . . . the list goes on!

The only way you can understand the messages you are given is to record them, analyze them, and finally, learn from them. For instance, if you recognize a feeling in your stomach, try and analyze it at the time. What does it feel like—good or bad? What does it remind you of? Pin the emotion down: excitement, anticipation, nervousness, anxiety, anger, fear, and so on. If you take the time to recall, you will find you can liken what you're feeling to a previous experience of that emotion—but only in taking the time to contemplate your awareness can you learn and benefit from the messages you receive.

As events unfold, go back through your diary to see if your messages were correct; learn from your success and your failures. Always leave a space after you've recorded your thoughts; later, go back and write what happened and the date (a red pen is good for this, so it stands out.) You will be amazed at the information you receive, once you start this process—for, in effect, you're letting your subconscious know that you're ready to listen. Together with using Tarot, you are outlining a method for communicating with your intuition and, therefore, it responds.

This is an entire subject in itself and, as I have already mentioned, it is very much a personal experience. For instance, whenever I "see" a rose, it represents love being given; for a friend it always represents a birth, and for yet another it represents a funeral! So you see, I really don't want to compromise your intuition with a set of "rules." Intuition is a very personal experience; however, the information you now have is certainly sufficient for you to understand your own development.

Tying it all together

I can almost hear you reminding me that I said you don't need a "special gift" to read Tarot. This is true, but the fact remains that anyone who seriously works with the Tarot cannot prevent his or her psychic development from unfolding. It's like an occupational hazard. Everyone has the ability to open their awareness and to develop this side of their self, but most people are just so busy that they miss the signs.

By working with Tarot, you have selected your chosen "tool" to express the language you share with your subconscious mind, your intuition, and the universe. In the stillness of the moment that you cast your cards, you follow a concentrated ritual, from spreading your cloth, shuffling your cards, focusing upon your question, to cutting the deck. This process is a form of meditation in itself when done correctly, which helps us to attune as we open ourselves up to higher guidance.

Psychic development is a personal journey. There is no set pace, for it is different for everyone, but I felt it only right to inform you of the various experiences you may encounter. None of which, I must add, is frightening—in fact, it's quite uplifting as you begin to recognize it.

This was how I first started providing guidance and teaching others. Quite a number of people started coming to me for help because they were experiencing odd things that they didn't understand and didn't feel they could speak about to anyone else they knew. I introduced them to the same diary technique and it works very well.

So your Tarot diary has many functions:

- It substantially increases retention of information as you learn your cards (ninety percent rather than ten percent)
- It provides a reference to reflect and study your readings later
- It helps you to be objective with self-readings
- It provides a record for comparing your original interpretation to the actual outcome of the situation, thus fine-tuning your understanding
- It helps build your confidence to read for others as you start to see the results from your own readings
- It enables you to understand, link, and integrate your psychic development and intuition with your Tarot

These may seem like simple steps, but the diary is highly effective and your most powerful development tool.

Just Before We Begin . . .

I feel it is a great pity that a number of people learn the major
arcana and then, because they feel they can do readings with
these alone, miss out on the minor arcana. These cards provide
essential details to the reading, so please avoid this trap. I believe
the minor arcana is actually easier to learn and so we will cover
it first, followed by the court cards and then the major arcana.

With the Gilded Tarot, you will see that each of the cards
has a color key, shown like a jewel on the borders of the card.
These correspond to the element that the suit represents,
which acts as an excellent memory jogger when you're just
getting started:

Minor Arcana
Wands = Red = Fire
Cups = Gold = Water
    (Water is colorless and therefore reflects the container)
Swords = Blue = Air
Pentacles = Green = Earth

All the major arcana cards have a black color key on their borders.

As we cover the meaning of each card, place it in front of you, leaving the others face down so they don't distract you, and take a moment to allow the images of the card to mingle with the interpretations suggested. Allow yourself to sink into the picture of the card. Don't rush this part or you'll miss a vital connection with your deck. Don't just read the meaning of the card; take a moment to read the description, for within this is the actual meaning itself—the symbolism that creates the interpretation.

The interpretations that follow show the essence of the meaning, but also allow room for you to expand your own thoughts within the framework of the meanings given and, therefore, to make them your own in your diary.

One card does not a reading make

As we are going to cover each of the cards individually in a moment, it seems relevant to inform you that the important factor, and perhaps the art (the secret, if you will) of reading Tarot is through the association of the cards to one another.

This is why learning the cards one by one, in parrot fashion, would prove unhelpful, for as the cards combine, their respective energies merge. If you've ever had an "automated reading" on the Internet, this may explain why they often don't appear to make a great deal of sense.

By all means, learn the interpretations for each card, but realize that the accuracy of the reading, and therefore the ultimate interpretation, lies in how the cards relate to one another once they are laid out into a spread. Your conscious mind and your subconscious work together, as if composing the answers to a crossword puzzle. The images immediately register with your subconscious, while your conscious mind provides the links.

In all readings, you will look for confirmation of your interpretations from the other cards. For instance, if you have one card that can represent marriage, you would look for confirmation from other cards to strengthen this. This is another area in which a lot of people go wrong in learning Tarot. It is important to learn each card, but one must realize that the surrounding cards can alter or modify the meaning.

There is a comparison here, a similarity worth mentioning even if you don't understand the subject. In astrology, each planet has an influence on another when they are in certain proximity. Planets are considered to be friendly, neutral, or enemies to one another. The "planetary war" that exists between them, in various combinations, provides the final interpretation.

Likewise, the cards have an effect upon one another. This can perhaps explain why, when you look at the individual meanings, you will find a similarity in some of the interpretations. This strengthens all cards by association. Sometimes it is subtle, but your subconscious will make the connection, passing it to your conscious mind to give you one of those "Aha!" moments. I will discuss card associations more deeply in the relevant sections as we progress.

About reversed cards

You are probably beginning to realize that there is more than one meaning to any given card. In addition, some people also interpret the cards differently when they appear upside down—known as reversals.

Again, this is an area of personal choice; some readers do and some don't.

I have tried both methods, and I don't use reversals, for I feel the cards offer enough interpretations if their associations are read correctly, considering the myriad of combinations that can appear. If a card turns up reversed, I simply place it in an upright position.

For many people, a reversed card represents a block to the original interpretation, rather than a completely opposite meaning. If the area of reversals interests you, it may be something you wish to experiment with later, but for the purpose of our studies we will read all the cards as upright.

About Tarot spreads

Tarot spreads are a pattern of laying out the cards, in which each position has a designated meaning and the card is interpreted in relation to its position. However, it makes sense that you need to understand the card's meaning first—so we will cover spreads once we conclude the individual meanings.

Getting started

- Please lay out your reading cloth and withdraw the relevant card as we cover it, leaving the others face down so the images don't distract you.
- Allow yourself to study the card, and see how the images relate to the interpretations.
- Hold the card in your fingers and allow yourself to feel its energy.
- Open your diary and, on the first page, write the name of the card and today's date. Write down bullet points for the meaning of the card, as you say the meaning out loud.
- Now you need to personalize your experience of the card, which will make it more real for you. Consider your own life experiences and make a list of personal circumstances in which this card would have been ap-

propriate, past or present. You don't need to labor over this; allow your thoughts to flow freely and don't be afraid to write them down—there is no right or wrong.

- Next, extend your awareness outside yourself. Consider friends, family, or acquaintances who may have encountered the experience of this card. Did someone immediately spring to mind as you read the card meaning? Make a list of those people and their situations.

I recommend that you leave some room on the page to return to later, as you will find your awareness has been opened and your subconscious will begin to quietly work at the seeds you have planted, bringing further incidents to mind as you go about your normal daily life. You will find you observe events around you differently.

At the end of each day, add your relevant comments based on your observations—it doesn't matter how small, so long as you add something. This can be on the corresponding page to begin with but, as you progress, just make a new entry with the date and record any events that happened to you that you can relate to certain cards.

The purpose of your diary is to record events in Tarot language, for within the Tarot lies every conceivable event that fills our lives and the lives of those around us. By doing this, the messages of the Tarot will become real for you.

Your diary is not only a learning tool; it is also important that you be able to look back and see how you have progressed, so you can recognize your achievement over a period of time. We will cover further benefits of your diary when we start doing spreads—but please use it as we cover each item.

Following completion of each suit

Once you have written something for each card, from Ace through Ten of the individual suits, please lay the cards out in a row, as follows:

Follow the suit across, noting the progression. Go through the individual meanings of each card, noticing the different moods, images, and energies. This is a good exercise you can do at any time, as it will help you to recognize the energy of the element represented and the different forms it can take.

Congratulations

If you've stayed with me so far, you've successfully concluded the all-important foundations to learning Tarot! Now, let's go and meet the individual cards.

Summary of your working tools

- Gilded Tarot deck
- Protective pouch or box to store your Tarot cards when not in use
- A black reading cloth (approximately twenty-four inches square) on which to lay your cards
- A small natural quartz crystal, programmed for guidance and protection
- Your diary to record information and experiences as you progress

---

Meeting
the Tarot

Part Two

The Minor Arcana—Suit of Wands

Wands represent the element of fire, the spark of creativity that inspires us to take action. They stand for self-expression through enterprise, so they frequently refer to work and business. Fire is an active, male energy.

Ace of Wands

ACE OF WANDS

All the aces represent new beginnings but wands are also initiators, so this card represents a dynamic and driving energy force.

Note the fire blazing from this magical ornate wand, suspended in the sky. A pair of male hands appears to nurture the wand, tentatively, almost reverently, reaching toward it.

It represents the beginning of action and taking initiative, being creative in enterprise, the birth of new ideas and inspirations, and can also represent the seed of a new life.

The Ace of Wands symbolizes the seeds of an idea that you feel very excited about; this frequently has a career or business orientation. A new job or the start of a new business venture are typical situations around which this card appears. As there is a great deal of creative energy indicated with this card, it is extremely good for anyone involved in creative endeavors.

Due to the element it represents, this card indicates a high degree of energy and action, so it holds a force of strength, enthusiasm and excitement . . . all the ingredients required at the outset to make a venture successful! Any projects started under the auspices of this card hold good promise for the future.

It can also represent an entirely new way of life, with the anticipation and excitement that such a transition would bring.

If accompanied by the Empress, it almost always brings news of a pregnancy or birth—literally the creation of a new life, since the Ace of Wands is a male active energy, which is also associated with procreation, the seed of life.

If a new relationship is indicated and the Ace of Wands also presents itself, you can be assured that it is going to be quite a passionate relationship!

As with every reading, remember: *how* the card's energies will be expressed can be identified from the other cards surrounding it.

Two of Wands

We see a young man facing two wands that are now firmly placed in the ground, showing that his project has become more established. He looks between them, far beyond into the horizon, contemplating his future plans. The vegetation is healthy, lush, and vibrant, which brings a sense of optimism. The two deer gazing back at him, with equal contemplation, mirror the two wands.

Two can symbolize the possibility of outside influence, perhaps in the form of a partnership. The fork in the road shows future choices and decisions that will need to be made as the querent progresses.

Having moved forward from the energy and ideas that the Ace brought, the Two of Wands shows that the initial stages have progressed to get the project off the ground. While the Ace is a wonderful card in theory, it cannot become significant if the energy is not manifested into reality.

As with all new ventures, you need to focus on your future plans and put in the required amount of effort to succeed. But the presence of this card shows that the potentiality exists.

The energy of the Two may also indicate a partnership; collaborations and negotiations with others may be significant to your project, so these are worthy of consideration.

The Two of Wands is a positive card that shows you moving in the direction of your goals and ambitions.

THREE OF WANDS

Three of Wands

It could be that we are looking at the same man in this scene, but note the difference in his attire. His robes are certainly a step up from those he wore in the Two of Wands. His hair is perhaps longer, symbolizing some passage of time, and his stance appears more confident. The two wands are now positioned behind him, showing work completed. The third wand he holds aloft as he gazes out to sea.

It may be that the ship he views is setting sail, or he could be waiting for his ship to come in—either way, his thoughts are still focused upon the future. Note the three seagulls—like his goals and ideas, they stretch equally between him and the ship.

We see a positive pattern of progression emerging here, taking the initial energy from the Ace, then manifesting the idea and now a completion of those first steps. Your initial goals have been realized, and while these have been successful there is still more work ahead.

The Three of Wands indicates progress, initial success, and yet even more planning to keep everything forward moving and heading in the right direction.

Four of Wands

Four wands, firmly planted in the ground, show the stability of the number four. Garlands of flowers have been attached, signifying triumph and celebrations. In this card a man now faces us; his attention is upon his family and he appears contented. Rabbits graze peacefully, undisturbed, in a serene atmosphere.

We now see stability as a result of the hard work that has gone before. Not only feeling satisfied with what you have so far accomplished but also a sense of harmony—which now means you can afford to reward yourself with some time off. Holidays are indicated, a time of rest and relaxation with your family and those you love, a welcome pause to recharge your batteries.

The Four of Wands brings a feel-good factor into play, a sense of contentment with oneself and life.

When other indications are present, it can also show plans for marriage being made—in which case, this card would further strengthen the message of the other cards.

Five of Wands

We can see five men threatening one another with five wands, as if in combat, yet it is quite unclear as to who is fighting with whom. The sky appears unsettled in the background and two mice scurry away as if anticipating trouble. Five is a number of instability, change, and uncertainty.

The Five of Wands represents conflicts, differences of opinions, and petty squabbling.

These may not be large problems and they can be overcome if cooperation is sought. However, petty disorder can easily get out of hand and drain energy away from key issues that need to be resolved.

If this situation emerges around you, try not to become involved, for if it is handled correctly the turmoil will just blow over. Don't be tempted to add flames to the fire—if you can play diplomat, you may find yourself quite popular with colleagues at a later date.

If you need receptivity, then now is *not* the time to present your latest great idea to others, as there is the likelihood of power struggles and competition. Keep it in your drawer for another day when the energy is more conducive!

Six of Wands

Amidst waving banners and cheering crowds, a well-clad man rides proudly upright on his decorated steed. The wand he carries bears a laurel wreath, signifying success. The number six represents harmony and balance.

This lovely card signifies that your efforts and achievements will be recognized by others. As such, it can often show a promotion coming in your direction.

If you've been working hard, wondering if your efforts are ever going to pay off, then you can be assured that you will feel a sense of satisfaction with your accomplishments; furthermore, others will be pleased for you, too.

This type of success is well-deserved and you have every right to feel pleased with your efforts so far.

The Six of Wands is the bearer of great news.

Seven of Wands

A man holding a wand defends his position against six others. The open doorway he appears to defend may represent his home—therefore, he is defending his own ideals. His expression is one of great concentration, although he does not appear perturbed. Sevens show the completion of a cycle and can bring changes.

Your ideas or beliefs may be challenged, sufficiently for you to feel the need to defend your position. While you may meet with opposition, the Seven of Wands indicates that you can win through in this situation and overcome any obstacles put before you. To do so, you need to remain calm, have confidence in yourself, and possess the courage to stand up for what you believe in.

Eight of Wands

Eight wands fly through the air, indicating speed, over a fertile and lush countryside.

If you have experienced setbacks or delays, then the Eight of Wands will be a welcome sight, for this card always brings a swift-moving energy into play.

With this card comes a sudden burst of activity and excitement, following the arrival of good news.

The Eight of Wands can also represent travel, often by air.

Nine of Wands

NINE OF WANDS

A man dressed for battle guards eight wands; the ninth he holds before him in readiness to fight, defend, and protect that which he has worked so hard for. We can see by his pose and expression that he is weary, yet still he bravely protects his position. Nine is the penultimate number of the suit.

When the Nine of Wands presents itself, it tends to show that you feel as if all your energy has been spent. The road has been long and you just don't feel as if you can go another step. . . okay, now let's just stop there for a moment!

Although you may feel on the verge of giving up, the message that the Nine of Wands brings is that your success is closer than you think and that you do actually have the inner strength required to make it. This isn't the time to stop. Having come so far, *now* is the moment to gather all your reserves for the final push. Perseverance is the key—with courage and determination, your triumphant moment awaits you!

Ten of Wands

A man carries ten wands awkwardly into the night; his back is under strain from the weight he carries. He looks weary but his head is lifted, showing he has not given up and continues with determination. The Ten is the full expression of the suit.

You may feel weary and overwhelmed with responsibilities, or feel overburdened and under pressure and strain.
However, there are easier ways to handle the load, if you can take a step back and look beyond it, but determination will be required.

There could also be a warning here—that which began as a wonderful idea or project may now feel as if it has become a burden. This could represent overworking and therefore a reminder that balance in life is required.

Be careful of taking on more than you can deal with at this time, for you could regret it later.

The Minor Arcana—Suit of Cups

Cups represent water, which symbolizes the emotions, most particularly love and relationships. Water is a female, passive, and nurturing element.

Ace of Cups

A beautifully ornate golden cup magically sits afloat on the water—representing feelings and emotions. The phases of the moon, also symbolic of our emotions, is shown in the heavens. A large eye gazes upon the cup with three golden streams of light pouring from it to the cup; this could symbolize our three levels of being: physical, emotional, and spiritual—the recognition that love is the pure energy that can fill us on every level.

The Ace of Cups is often referred to as the Holy Grail.

Aces symbolize new beginnings, the water element represented by Cups stands for emotions, and so the Ace of Cups shows the start of a new relationship, the beginning of love and happiness.

For those already in a solid relationship, it represents a sense of renewal in the love partnership or the start of something new, which brings emotional happiness to the home and family.

With other indications, the Ace of Cups can also represent the birth of a child, since the element of water is female, which is receptive, nurturing, and life-giving.

If you consider how the senses are so intoxicated and enchanted when wrapped in a new romance, it gives an indication of the emotional euphoria that can be associated with this card.

Since the state of "bliss" is recognized as a state of being found through the energy of real love, it is an emotion all of humanity tends to seek. Whether romantically in the search for another, or spiritually in the form of enlightenment, it can therefore be likened to the search for the Holy Grail, that which we seek for fulfillment on an emotional level.

TWO OF CUPS

Two of Cups

A man and woman gaze into one another's eyes with undivided attention. The blond woman and brown-haired man represent the combination of the two opposite polarities. Note the bright light in the heavens extending down in a ring, encompassing the male and female, alighting upon each cup, which appears to draw and hold them together. This is the card of union. The Ace has now progressed into two energies, male and female.

The energy of the Ace has now manifested into reality, finding expression in the form of the Two of Cups.

This beautiful card is always a welcome sight with regard to romantic relationships. When the Two of Cups appears, it shows growth in a relationship; whatever the stage you have reached together, it represents moving to the next level.

For some (and with the indications of surrounding cards) this can represent commitment, engagement, or marriage—either way, it is an important union.

With the Two of Cups, the relationship is surrounded by an atmosphere of harmony, balance, kindness, and a silent understanding that words cannot express. Such is the delight of this bond, that somehow life cannot be imagined without the other. You are deliciously intoxicated and the feeling is mutual.

With the wonderful energy of this card, if there have been quarrels or disputes between loved ones, then the Two of Cups can bring reconciliation and rediscovery of the emotions that originally held this unity together.

Three of Cups

THREE OF CUPS

Three young women dance in the sky with streamers and sparkling light. The colors they are dressed in represent the other elements: green for earth, blue for air, and red for fire. Before them two cups pour water into a third that overflows, with two further streams of water flowing into the pool upon which it stands. We can see that two energies combined have created a third.

Water is the symbol of our emotions and in this instance our cup is overflowing.

There is emotional happiness together with a sense of abundance and achievement. The Three of Cups represents celebrations with friends and family; it can also indicate weddings or christenings.

The Three of Cups may also show the progress of a relationship that is emotionally fulfilling, a happy conclusion to matters, victory, and abundance. Generally, it tends to indicate reasons to celebrate with others.

Four of Cups

Three cups stand upright in the fore-ground while a fourth is magically offered from the clouds to the young man, who appears bored and unaffected by such an amazing event. He sits amidst a vibrant landscape, yet he seems lost within his own thoughts.

A mood of nonchalance surrounds the Four of Cups, an air of indifference. It can represent a feeling of boredom or inward discontent, even though nothing appears to actually be wrong.

You need to be watchful that, due to this mood, you don't inadvertently miss new invitations or opportunities—the kind of thing you'd kick yourself for later!

Five of Cups

FIVE OF CUPS

It is easy to feel the sense of anguish and dejection being experienced by the knight in this picture. With his head bowed and three spilled cups before him, he does not see the two upright cups still standing behind him. The moody colors of the sky reflect the atmosphere. Five stands for instability and change.

When the Five of Cups is drawn, it shows that you may be experiencing feelings of disappointment. Others may have let you down or you feel in some way betrayed. You may be recounting previous actions with some regret at how things have turned out, either due to your own actions or of those around you.

Perhaps a lover or trusted friend was not all you had hoped them to be. For this reason, this card can *sometimes* indicate the loss of a relationship and the natural process of grieving emotions that accompanies such an event.

Due to the emotional feelings that surround you, your logical mind is presently clouded. So be aware that at this stage the realities of the situation cannot be fully understood, nor appreciated, while the emotional process is being experienced.

In the card, three cups are spilled but two still remain standing, indicating that there are still positive factors at work which you have not yet seen, as your focus is currently held upon that which you feel you have lost.

It is important to read this card in context with the rest of the reading. Are there indications that the situation can be healed? Alternatively, it may show that it leads to something new and better ahead.

Please exercise care with this card, for I have known many occasions where it appeared that all was lost and yet it only represented a temporary situation that was later successfully resolved, or one that only existed in the client's mind and how he or she felt about a situation. This has also been true for me, on more than one occasion!

Six of Cups

Children happily play in a meadow surrounded by six cups filled with flowers. The children represent aspects of our past and pleasant memories. Six is the number of harmony and balance.

The Six of Cups indicates something or someone from the past coming back. This can be an old friend making an entrance, or the revival of an old love relationship.

It may also represent situations from the past resurfacing and being brought back to you. In this instance, it would be something that affected you emotionally, perhaps something you feel passionate about—so it is not strictly limited to your love life.

Whatever it may be, this "blast from the past" will make an entrance now and it could bring you happiness and satisfaction.

Traditionally, this card also indicated nostalgia—being stuck in the past and not moving forward—but it would need to be badly aspected and supported by surrounding cards.

By the way, you will notice that I sometimes refer to a card as being either well aspected or badly aspected. These are terms I use to describe the effects of other cards on a card by their *association* to it. For example, a card that is well aspected would be one surrounded by cards that are considered very positive. The merging energies therefore have a beneficial effect on that card, with the opposite being the case for a card that is badly aspected.

Seven of Cups

SEVEN OF CUPS

Seven cups sit among the clouds and skim the water, each containing an interesting treasure; they all appear tempting and beckon to be chosen. The fact that they sit amid water and clouds represents our subconscious desires, or literally having one's "head in the clouds."

The Seven of Cups symbolizes a situation where you feel many choices are possible. You may feel overwhelmed as your imagination runs away with you. The difficulty lies in actually making a decision.

You need to look at the situation in a practical manner, view your choices realistically, and decide which path to pursue. The imagination can present things unrealistically, so the danger here is that if nothing is done you could find yourself left empty-handed! Therefore, exercise care; take a practical, methodical, and sensible approach in making your choice.

Eight of Cups

The figure in this card has his back turned away from the eight cups behind him. The cups appear to have previously been carefully stacked but some are now in disarray. The stance of the figure does not appear to be dejected; he is upright and resolute, gazing off into the distance, appearing ready to embark on a new journey and listening to his inner voice. The full moon represents the subconscious mind.

The word most associated with this card is "abandonment."

The eight cups are behind the figure, which represents the emotional investment given previously. Just as this card shows, you now turn your back on the situation and walk away from it, as it no longer fulfills you. Therefore, it shows abandoning something through disappointment.

It must be remembered that the action of walking away from the situation is a *choice*. Frequently this represents something that has held you back for a long time but, due to the amount of emotional investment, you found it difficult to walk away and move on, even though inwardly you may have been aware for some time that you felt disillusioned. Finally, a new path is pursued.

Nine of Cups

NINE OF CUPS

The jolly innkeeper greets and salutes us with a cup held high, while eight more upright cups sit neatly stacked upon full barrels, representing cheer and abundance.

The Nine of Cups is one of the most promising of the Tarot and is sometimes referred to as the "wish card," signifying the achievement of an important desire that brings you fulfillment.

It can represent emotional and material fulfilment, abundance—also sensual pleasures! It indicates you will feel well pleased.

Ten of Cups

TEN OF CUPS

The artist informs us that he envisioned this card from his own viewpoint, as he would see it when returning home, his family awaiting him. The landscape is peaceful and vibrant, the atmosphere harmonious. From the home, ten golden cups arch into the sky upon a rainbow.

The Ten of Cups is the ultimate card for the suit of love and happiness and provides more stability than the Nine. Romantics, this is the one you've been looking for—the perfect realization of emotional love.

When the Ten of Cups shows up in a reading, it represents happiness in one's home life, together with the promise of lasting success in a relationship. It symbolizes committed and contented love with permanence.

This card frequently appears when marriage is "in the cards."

STEP 8

The Minor Arcana—Suit of Swords

Swords represent the air element, which stands for the intellect, the thinking aspect of our self. This differs from the creative aspect of fire (wands), for air represents the more logical and analytical side of our thoughts and, therefore, is more discriminating. Our mind can be our greatest friend or our worst enemy, since our thoughts frequently get in our own ways, creating confusion, anxiety, and conflict. The suit of swords often represents struggle and animosity.

For this reason many people are rather fearful of the cards from this suit. However, there is no need to fear them. On the positive side, swords allow us to cut through confusion to see matters as they really are and then deal with the situation realistically and with great clarity. This cannot be accomplished without first seeing the truth of the matter.

Ace of Swords

Against the backdrop of a stormy sky, an ornate golden sword, encrusted with jewels, hangs in the heavens. Surrounded by a blue ribbon, the streamers symbolize triumph and celebration.

What a wonderfully powerful card this is! When the Ace of Swords appears, it signifies victory and triumph over difficulties. In order to do so, you will use great reserves of inner strength and clarity of thought, so your success is well deserved.

The Ace of Swords represents a great force of strength and inner power, showing you have the ability to overcome setbacks and adversity. This is a card of victory and triumph through one's own actions.

Two of Swords

We see a woman's face suspended against a cloudy night sky; a golden band covers her eyes and ears. Being blindfolded means she cannot see her present situation. Before her, two golden swords are crossed in front of the moon. The swords reflect the conflict of her thoughts; the moon represents her subconscious mind.

The Two of Swords symbolizes a stalemate situation, or one in which a deadlock exists. You may feel that you need to make a decision, yet are unable to move one way or another due to feelings of confusion.

We do not see the woman's hands, so it can be assumed she is free to remove the blindfold herself, but inertia prevents her from doing so.

You need to look at the situation logically and try a new approach to break the deadlock. There is *always* something that can be done. In the eyes of the Universe no decision is still a decision . . . so it's far better to take an active part in your destiny.

Three of Swords

THREE OF SWORDS

Three swords pierce a heart against the backdrop of a dark, stormy sky. But note how the clouds are stormy underneath yet clearing at the top of the card. The center of the heart is covered by an image of the sun; in astrology the sun is our outward appearance to the world.

Stormy emotions can lead to quarrels; should this escalate, it could lead to a separation. However, please remember this card still only has the energy of a three.

There may be upheaval in family situations, but hope for the future is shown in this card, represented by the clearing sky above the image.

The Three of Swords can represent separation between loved ones; this card can also appear for couples who are separated through distance, work, and so on, making them miserable, so it does not necessarily mean a relationship split.

Four of Swords

FOUR OF SWORDS

A knight rests upon his bed; the brick wall behind him shows the safety of his sanctuary. Above him three swords hang against a colored banner, while the fourth lies in readiness and within easy grasp of his hand, suggesting that at some point he will pick it up to battle once again.

The Four of Swords shows rest, recovery, and "recharging batteries" after a period of struggle, stress, or strain.

You may feel slightly detached from outside events, experiencing a need to retreat inside yourself for comfort, or you may just feel too weary to participate for the moment. A period of rejuvenation is needed, time to regroup one's resources before continuing onward again. Take some time out to replenish. This card can also indicate convalescence.

Five of Swords

In the breaking light of day, we witness what has been a battleground scene. A lone figure stands holding five swords in a victorious pose, appearing totally oblivious to the suffering and devastation of those around him. There are no flying banners here to signify him as a hero, nor his actions as any to celebrate.

The Five of Swords shows that an element of deceit may be at work. Someone is not being honest in their dealings; there may be a hidden agenda or some form of underhandedness.

It may represent something that is lost in an unfair manner, or perhaps someone leaving suddenly without any proper explanation or truth, showing insensitivity to those concerned.

As a card that can show dishonor, defeat, or loss, it warns you to be careful. It also indicates that selfish victories are short-lived, so you must also ensure that you operate in an ethical manner in all your undertakings.

Six of Swords

SIX OF SWORDS

By the light of the full moon a cloaked lady calmly ferries herself across the water. Six swords stand upright in the boat but they do not appear to be threatening.

The meaning of the Six of Swords is quite literal: moving out of stormy waters into calmer ones. If you have experienced difficult times, this card assures you that matters will improve and harmony will once more be restored.

As the six swords in the boat demonstrate, our experiences are part of us and travel with us, a reminder of the life lessons we have encountered.

This card can also represent a physical journey, usually long or over water.

Seven of Swords

The man leaving this scene appears to be up to no good. He glances backward as he makes his exit, carrying five swords awkwardly, having dropped two in his haste, which will no doubt be discovered.

The Seven of Swords can represent situations not going as you had anticipated or bad luck affecting matters.

Sometimes theft may be indicated, so you need to be mindful of this and take the necessary precautions. It can often show a situation where something is taken in greed, without any apparent feelings of guilt—such is usually the nature of theft. There is an element of unfairness surrounding this card, but forewarned is forearmed.

This card also represents the use of diplomacy against heavy-handed methods to achieve the desired result.

Eight of Swords

Against the backdrop of the night sky, we see a solitary woman with her eyes, ears, and wrists bound, surrounded by eight swords. Note how the swords do not touch her and the chain around her wrists appears to be loose. The light that emanates in a downward stream from the swords represents clarity of thought, which due to her blindfold she cannot see.

Feeling restricted, fear is preventing you from moving forward and your confidence may have taken a knock.

However, as the image shows, none of the swords actually touch the woman and only her bound senses are preventing her from moving out of the situation or seeing it clearly.

The advice of this card is to remain calm and strong, not to give in to feelings of paralysis in order to progress out of the situation. Bear in mind that the swords depicted in the card also represent clarity of thought and therefore the answer *is* available to you—perhaps you need to look at the situation differently.

Nine of Swords

The woman depicted in this card appears to be trying to comfort herself. She sits upright in bed as if a bad dream has awakened her, or perhaps she is unable to sleep due to her troubled thoughts— symbolized by the nine swords, crossed and suspended, before her. In the window, we see an owl observing her; owls are commonly associated with wisdom.

This card often shows feelings of suffering, disappointment, and despair, a sense of anxiety being experienced. Yet once more, we are reminded that the swords do not actually touch the person. It may be the fear of them that creates the problem and therefore the negative emotions can become self-perpetuating. Seeing the matter clearly (symbolized by the owl) releases you from it.

Usually, it is our fear that blinds us, making what "might" happen appear worse than the situation really is.

Although this card is similar to the Eight, there is more intensity with the Nine, showing a progression. For example, if the advice suggested by the Eight has not been followed, it could lead to the inner suffering as shown in the Nine of Swords.

Ten of Swords

TEN OF SWORDS

Ten swords hang directly above a motionless figure on the ground. A lone deer appears to be moving in the direction of the figure as if to investigate the scene. But against the dark scenery we can see light emanating from the swords. As the final card of this minor suit, it reminds us of the meaning of air—cutting through illusion to see matters as they really are, in order to move forward.

The Ten of Swords can represent a feeling of loss due to the ending of a difficult situation. Yet within this, we are released and ready for a new beginning, for life moves in cycles.

It can warn about ruined plans, or matters that don't materialize as hoped, leading to feelings of disappointment—but take comfort in the fact that perhaps they were just not meant to be.

If this card appears in a "future" position, it acts as a warning—the outcome is now dependent upon the actions you take to avert the situation. Action shapes destiny!

The Minor Arcana—Suit of Pentacles

Pentacles represent the element of earth, which symbolizes our physical being and the needs of our daily life, the material aspects that we work for and value—such as money, property, and material possessions. Earth is a stabilizing influence.

Ace of Pentacles

ACE OF PENTACLES

A large golden pentacle dominates this card. The surrounding countryside is green, healthy, and calm. The top of the pentacle sits squarely in the heavens, with the moon behind it and daylight breaking. An angle of the pentacle points to the earth, symbolic of the earthly element.

The Ace of Pentacles represents prosperity and material gains, the beginning of successful endeavors that bring good financial reward—so this would be an excellent card if you were looking to start a new business venture.

It can signify documents that hold material importance, such as company accounts, education certificates or diplomas, marriage contracts, inheritance documents such as wills, bank accounts, or house deeds. Sometimes it may represent an important letter being received, although frequently it would be of an official or monetary nature.

Together with supporting cards, it may indicate a lump sum of money, gifts, or an inheritance.

Two of Pentacles

A youth, wearing a look of calm concentration, juggles two pentacles, with a rainbow emanating from his hands. Behind him we can see a ship on a calm sea, silhouetted against a full moon with a dolphin. These symbols represent the world of our emotions; in this case they do not disturb our preoccupied youth in his task.

The Two of Pentacles represents the effort needed to successfully maintain a balance in life; this can be trying to keep more than one project going simultaneously, a balance of home and work, or even juggling finances.

Care is needed to maintain balance to ensure everything progresses smoothly and flows harmoniously. The signs are good that this can be attained.

Three of Pentacles

A young craftsman shows steady progress as he diligently works with pride and concentration. We see the tools of his trade and the result of his labors, which he holds in his hands admiringly.

The Three of Pentacles reveals that through your efforts, success is beginning to show. You should feel a sense of achievement now, along with some improvement materially.

This card can bring recognition for your work, either financially or through others acknowledging your talents and abilities, although usually in a more formal way that somehow rewards you. It also shows work that you enjoy and have a natural ability for.

Whatever activities it may represent, as a three it shows the initial stages of completion with successful attainment.

Four of Pentacles

A well-dressed merchant holds four pentacles tightly to his chest.

FOUR OF PENTACLES

The Four of Pentacles can indicate being focused upon goals and financial matters at this time and being prepared to work hard to attain them.

However, having worked hard to achieve some form of financial stability, there may now be a fear of loss, and this can lead to feeling the need to hold onto everything a bit too tightly. There is nothing wrong with working hard for one's money, or in being careful with one's resources—so long as it doesn't become a preoccupation.

This card frequently appears when there is an element of being overly cautious or "hanging back" emotionally, and may indicate that you need to let go a little in order to move the situation forward—taking a calculated risk.

Negatively aspected, it can indicate someone who has a miserly disposition, or does not feel inclined to share.

Five of Pentacles

A humbly dressed couple stand before a stained-glass window showing five pentacles. The woman holds her child close to provide warmth. Behind them is a church where they could seek shelter, but they appear so preoccupied by their fate that they do not see it.

This card is perhaps everything the merchant shown in the Four was worrying about! The Five of Pentacles supplies a warning of paying careful attention to your financial affairs to guard against loss, so this isn't the time to head for the shops and indulge in a spot of retail therapy!

Temporary hardships are indicated, and may be felt on a financial or even emotional level, yet help is at hand if you look more closely. Money or resources could be lacking, so take time to carefully review financial affairs, ensure everything is in order, and reorganize the budget accordingly.

This would not be a good time to enter into new financial commitments or agreements—let caution be your watchword here.

That said, be careful not to miss any valid opportunities that could improve your situation at this time.

Six of Pentacles

A well-dressed merchant holds the scales of balance and provides gold pentacles to outstretched hands.

The Six of Pentacles shows successful material gains and being in a position that allows you to share with others. Business ventures should be paying off, or perhaps a pay increase is coming in your direction.

It is important that once the work is done, the rewards are enjoyed. This is not only of a monetary nature but also a sign of sharing your time with others. Invariably, when we work hard, it is our nearest and dearest who pay the price of not having as much of our time as they deserve. Now that the results are beginning to manifest, show your appreciation, for time is a precious resource that can never be replaced.

If money has been outstanding, then this card indicates that it should now be received. The Six of Pentacles is a card of generosity and kindness, so gifts are also indicated.

Seven of Pentacles

SEVEN OF PENTACLES

A woman stands and takes a moment to assess her healthy crop before harvesting. She looks ahead to the future. The seven pentacles represent the financial gain she can now expect to receive from all her hard work and efforts, planting and nurturing her crop to this moment of fruition.

The Seven of Pentacles shows that hard work and patience will be rewarded and that working methodically toward accomplishment will bring success.

You should receive good news concerning your financial position at this time, and all forms of financial applications or sale negotiations are well aspected.

Although this is a good card, it is important to still plan for the future—once the harvest has been collected, it must be replenished for the next time.

Eight of Pentacles

By candlelight, a young man works with concentrated effort on the pentacle before him. Behind him are shown other pentacles as he perfects his skill. He appears to be working late into the night, showing dedication to his studies.

The Eight of Pentacles is often referred to as the "apprenticeship" card. It can signify learning a new skill or profession. As such, it frequently shows up when there is the offer of new employment or taking a new position. It can also show entrance to a learning establishment, such as a university or college, or even part-time study.

Quite often the Eight of Pentacles indicates that existing talents can be used to create a venture that will bring financial gains. This may be an interest, hobby, or additional ability that you are not currently using to its full potential.

This would be a good time to look into vocational matters more closely—if you have always wanted to follow a different career path (or advance your current one), then make some inquiries because the signs indicate the opportunity could be more accessible than you previously believed.

Nine of Pentacles

NINE OF PENTACLES

A woman is shown opulently adorned in beautiful clothes and jewels. She stands in front of an ornate gazebo in a garden that flourishes abundantly with nine pentacles. She views the falcon on her hand with a contented expression; the bird represents mastery of her goals and plans.

The Nine of Pentacles indicates financial success and material security, usually attained through one's own efforts. Although the woman in this card is depicted alone, the card symbolizes financial independence, not loneliness.

Finances should improve sufficiently to allow some comforts in life, and a pleasant and comfortable lifestyle. With other indications, this could represent an inheritance.

If you've been beavering away, working hard and carefully moving in the direction of your goals, then this card now brings the rewards for your efforts. Congratulations!

Ten of Pentacles

TEN OF PENTACLES

An open, sturdy wooden chest reveals ten golden pentacles. Families often used wooden chests to store their worldly treasures, before stashing them away for safety. The small furry creature looks well fed and appears pleased, while a turtle slowly ambles past, representing the unhurried passage of time. We see the symbol of the sun on the lid and front of the chest. In astrology, the sun often stands for the father figure, status, and honor.

The Ten of Pentacles signifies financial and family stability. Home and family security is central to this card and property sales are often indicated. It particularly tends to refer to the family home.

This card also shows material possessions being passed through the generations, so thought should be given to ensuring that wills, trusts, and insurance policies have been written, are in good order, and are up-to-date. Inheritances can also be indicated with this card.

It can represent large sums of money or an increase in finances, but should always be read in context with the other cards in its proximity.

This lovely card shows the satisfaction of feeling settled and materially secure. Your home and family have a firm and comfortable foundation . . . all is well in your world.

STEP 10

About the Court Cards

Of all the cards, it is perhaps the court cards that offer so many differing interpretations, which may explain why some people find them challenging to learn. By reference, some of the meanings can represent a person, an event, or even different aspects of the same person. Little wonder they cause confusion! However, what I present to you here has clear boundaries; it is how the interpretations of the courts have evolved for me over the years, a format that I find works successfully.

Firstly, the most important point is to relate the relevant courts to the element of the suit that they represent, which signifies the kind of energy influencing them.

If you lay the court cards out in front of you and then reread the meaning of the suit element first, before looking at each individual interpretation, you will find this helpful.

The meanings I have provided for you are exactly the way I use them myself and they have always given me reliable results.

Personally, I do not identify people symbolized by the courts with astrology signs, as I have found this to be too limiting. It can sometimes be quite representational of a person's Sun sign, but many individuals have strong characteristics from their rising sign and Moon. Not only this, but the client may not know the astrology sign of the person that you refer to. So I don't use this basis.

Similarly, I don't make reference to the physical coloring, complexion, eye color, or hair color (which can be dyed) of the card either. I feel a person's character and personality traits are more reliable.

If you think about it, when we describe a person to a friend, we tend to use a few brief words or phrases that typify them, to draw a picture of the type of person they are. We do this all the time. Identifying the court cards you will find is really just the same. I have found that in a reading, I can give a few descriptive phrases and the client usually identifies who the person is quite quickly—if not, we know it is someone still to enter the scene.

In the descriptions that follow, you will find those provided for the kings and queens to be quite lengthy. This is to further expand upon the type of personality you may find associated with this card and in various settings. People do not have to fit every possible variation, but you will find the basic characteristics do not change.

When considering who these cards represent, it is also important to realize that, as a balanced individual, we all show some characteristics of each element; for women, it is possible for each queen, for example, to represent a different side of ourselves, dependent on circumstances. However, when considering the courts, it is important to look for the card that is most representative of a person, more than the others—and this isn't actually too difficult to do.

A good exercise for putting this into practice is to study the courts first and then, in your diary, list people who instantly come to mind for each of the court cards.

People or Events?

Some of the court cards can represent a person or an event. This perhaps is where the confusion begins, but please don't concern yourself for the moment, as once more this comes down to associations with other cards and will be explained.

In relation to people:

- *Pages:* Children or young people of either sex, up to around seventeen years of age.
- *Knights:* Young men of around eighteen to mid-twenties.
- *Queens:* Mature women, usually from eighteen years.
- *Kings:* Mature men, thirty-plus, but sometimes from eighteen upward.

For me, the knights almost always represent events, as opposed to people. This could be due to the fact that young people are regarded as "adults" at a much younger age nowadays, compared to ancient times when young men took apprenticeships, were judged based on seniority among their peers, and "earned" their respect.

Women, however, reach childbearing age quite young, are usually psychologically more mature than males, and therefore move from child to adult quite quickly.

In relation to events:

- *Pages:* Bring messages containing news.
- *Knights:* Represent forms of action, expressed with different energies representative of the suit, and certain events.

So that you can compare the different energies and character-istics of the court cards, we will cover each of them in groups of "rank"—i.e., all the pages, then knights, queens, and kings, instead of grouping them by their relevant suit. I feel it is far easier to note the differences between the individuals and the elements this way. You will notice a strong connective theme with the personalities that share the same suits—only subtly different due to maturity, or masculine versus feminine energy.

Once more, as you cover the individual cards, have each one in front of you and then log it in your diary with its mean-ings. Then write down any people (or events) where appropri-ate, in order to make the cards real for you, rather than just a piece of card stock with printed words and pictures.

One point to note . . .

One particular aspect of the Gilded Tarot is that you will find the court "families" all surrounded by, or dressed in, the col-ors that represent their suit. With wands we have red, the fire element; gold for cups, the water element; blue for swords, the air element; and green for pentacles, the earth element.

Take a moment to place the court cards side by side, in groups of four, together in their respective suits. If you lay them all out in rows from left to right you can immediately recognize the different feeling related to each suit and the sense of uniformity within each family (page, knight, queen, and king). This is an extremely helpful exercise that will help you identify them quickly and effectively when they appear in a spread.

STEP II

The Minor Arcana—The Pages

In days of old, pages were of a young age and often acted as messengers, delivering by hand sealed messages on behalf of their king or queen, in the royal court.

Page of Wands

PAGE OF WANDS

Child or young person (fire element):

Active and energetic, cheerful, optimistic, sometimes appears quite fearless, action oriented. Full of new ideas but often lacks "thinking it through," tendency to dive into things headfirst without much forethought. "Cheeky little monkey" or "lovable rogue" describes this person.

As an event:

Good news coming in—usually swiftly, may be work-related. Can be classed as letters, telephone calls, or word of mouth.

Page of Cups

Child or young person (water element):

Kind, thoughtful, gentle, creative, artistic, generally well-behaved, polite. Sensitive to others but can also be slightly over-sensitive to criticism or harsh realities of life. Usually well-liked by others but may have difficulty socially at school, due to sensitive nature and other children's thought-less words or actions taken to heart.

As an event:

Happy news of an emotional nature generally; can be news about love, engagement, marriage, or birth.

Page of Swords

Child or young person (air element):

Quick-minded, cool, deep. Takes everything in but doesn't speak unnecessarily. Secretive, analytical, tends to make logical decisions, appears quite solemn even when happy. Can appear insensitive to others' feelings. Injustice on any level upsets them as they stick to the rules and can't understand others who don't. Can be deceitful or gossipy, causing rumors and trouble, though not intentionally.

As an event:

Represents delayed news or disappointing news. It can show (minor) problems with or for a child—e.g., a child's behavior. Depending upon the surrounding cards, it may represent someone causing minor problems with petty gossip.

Page of Pentacles

Child or young person (earth element):

Studious or academic child who enjoys studying and learning. A solid young person, methodical in his or her approach, hardworking, well-behaved, polite, self-disciplined, with love and respect for animals and the countryside. A solid individual, not a "party animal" type. They are usually good with their hands or anything of a practical nature.

As an event:

You should receive some good news that will bring welcome changes into your life; this may have a financial or academic connection.

The Minor Arcana—The Knights

All the knights represent some form of action; this is easy to relate to when you note they are all on horseback, sufficiently suited up, and ready for action. The energy and type of action, or how it will be expressed, is in keeping with the element that they represent.

Knight of Wands

The Knight of Wands sets out with confidence. He tends to bring swift movement to matters with a high level of energy.

If representing a young man (fire element):

When representing a young man, the Knight of Wands is energetic, adventurous, full of ambitious ideas, warm, and exciting, but apt to be a little hasty.

As an event:

The Knight of Wands almost always shows when someone is about to change residence. May also signify a long journey being taken (sometimes both, as in immigration). As always, look for supporting cards.

The energy this knight represents tends to make clients feel they must act quickly, as it has a high level of creative energy—but they must not, in their haste, forget to check all the details first.

Knight of Cups

The Knight of Cups, in his beautiful robes, sets forth with idealistic expectation. With suitable theatrical expression he holds his cup high, amid streamers of celebration upon his rearing horse. The vision of our romantic knight . . .

If representing a young man (water element):

As a young man, he would be romantic and idealistic.

As an event:

The energy this knight symbolizes is always felt on an emotional level. He represents offers being brought to you that will be accompanied by a high level of excitement.

Due to the element he represents, the Knight of Cups is the one to look for in relation to romantic invitations or proposals of marriage. For those in the arts, he often brings interesting work developments or offers (card associations determine which).

Knight of Swords

This knight is the only one showing his sword, representing his ability to take fearless action. His sword is raised to an observant owl, representing wisdom. The job of the Knight of Swords is to teach us to use discernment, to see things as they really are, and to have the strength to deal with them appropriately. Since doing so is difficult when we feel highly charged emotionally, it can create feelings of turmoil instead.

If representing a young man (air element):

As a young man, he would be quick-minded, rather serious, and sometimes impatient. He has a strong character and can be strangely magnetic, yet sometimes appears insensitive to the feelings of others, due to his forthright manner.

As an event:

The energy brought by this knight is so swiftly moving that it may feel chaotic, due to the speed at which events unfold and the feelings of confusion this could create. Sometimes his swift-moving action is a necessary requirement, as it brings about better circumstances. There is a great deal of strength offered by this knight, which can be advantageous, so you need to be ready to ride with the changes he brings.

Knight of Pentacles

KNIGHT OF PENTACLES

The Knight of Pentacles doesn't appear to be going anywhere, for his horse stands quietly in a meadow, observed by an undisturbed rabbit.

The movement this knight brings is always of a welcome nature, for the Knight of Pentacles never cuts corners, due to his methodical approach. The children's tale of the race between the hare and the tortoise is a good example.

He may not appear as exciting as the other knights, but he can be relied upon to always bring results in the end.

If representing a young man (earth element):
As a young man, he would be steady and trustworthy—Mr. Reliable.

As an event:
Everyone is always pleased to see this card, for it means that something one has been waiting for finally comes through—and this can relate to any area of life, whether work, money, or love. If you have a situation that you have methodically developed and patiently waited for and as yet have seen no results, you will find them forthcoming at last!

The Minor Arcana—The Queens

The queens represent females of the element of their suit. Since more women are independent nowadays, working mothers and wives, the traditional interpretations are slightly different.

The first paragraph concentrates on the main personality traits of this woman, by which she can normally be identified. This has then been expanded to provide further indications of the type.

Queen of Wands

The Queen of Wands has a warm, attractive personality, generally cheerful and always busy with a number of different projects at any given time.

Her home is important to her; she is loyal to and protective of family and friends, the one they can count on. Nothing is too much trouble for her. Note the fire burning in the background of this card—reminiscent of "keeping the home fires burning."

QUEEN OF WANDS

If this woman were a full-time mother, you would still find her volunteering at the school fair, ferrying others' children to and from school, and running other errands in between! She has endless energy and thrives on being busy.

At work her desk would look like merry chaos, but she can find everything. She's the one flying round with the clipboard, energetic, organizing everyone else, full of ideas, cheerfully encouraging others into action. She can be quite ambitious and certainly has the energy and drive to ensure she succeeds but, because she's always so busy, packing everything into her twenty-four hours, she can tend to lack detail and her chaos can make her forgetful—quantity rather than quality. But this aspect of herself is usually humorously forgiven due to her helpful and cheerful nature.

In the negative, this queen *may* be hot tempered, disorganized, controlling, or smothering. She can be vengeful, though not in an up-front manner; there may be tendency to "cattiness."

Queen of Cups

QUEEN OF CUPS

The Queen of Cups is kind, gentle, sensitive, and thoughtful, charming, socially polite, creative, and artistic. She sometimes can appear "switched off" from the outside world, as she is quite in tune with her inner world, which she can easily slip into, giving her a detached air at times. She prefers one-to-one friends or conversations, rather than large groups. Usually quite feminine and empathic by nature, she can at times be melancholy, or prone to shifting moods.

In the card, note her detached and distant expression.

The Queen of Cups likes things to be aesthetically pleasing; her home and her clothes and accessories all carry some small, fancy little detail that sets them apart. However understated, you will find tell-tale signs of this everywhere you look: her pen, her diary, items on her desk, and so on. Her home and clothing show taste and a touch of artistic flair—no matter what her budget—and her home is a place that reflects this sense of harmony she needs.

The Queen of Cups is the one who notices when someone doesn't appear themselves, as she's very sensitive to others' feelings. She would not force herself upon others, tending to be somewhat restrained in her nature, but if she is a good friend of yours, then she will spend hours listening to your problems, empathizing, offering support, and well-thought-out suggestions.

Whereas the Queen of Wands would be happy to do something practical for you (unlike this queen), she can also appear dismissive with her cheery attitude and would probably comment that she's sure everything will be fine in the end, or that she doesn't know what to suggest. Note the difference between the two elements. You would feel with the Queen of Cups as if someone really listened and cared.

The Queen of Cups is frequently found in the helping/caring/healing professions: nursing, teaching, alternative therapies, psychics, the arts, interior design, fashion, and so on.

Romantically, these people can be hurt easily, due to their sensitive nature. As they get older and learn from these experiences, you may find they become quite protective of themselves, and so may appear difficult to fathom, or seem aloof—but they are protecting the sensitive core of their emotions. Gentleness, kindness, and a sense of security are required in their relationships; harsh words or actions cut deep.

In the negative, they may be dreamy and unrealistic, overly sensitive, prone to a victim mentality, give up too easily (so not very "gritty"), be easily led by others, and can be manipulative. They dislike speaking out, seeing doing so as confrontational.

QUEEN OF SWORDS

Queen of Swords

The Queen of Swords is an independent woman who takes a no-nonsense approach. Her forthright manner can make her seem unemotional. However, she has a strong sense of fair play with a good reasoning mind and excellent perception, so she has mastered the ability to put emotion aside to concentrate on logic and facts.

Note how she holds her sword to the illumination of the light in this card—symbolic of the wisdom and clarity of thought swords can bring.

Traditionally, the Queen of Swords represented a woman on her own, who had known suffering and loss: widowed, divorced, or long single, and sometimes childless. However, this is not always the case and the personality traits are the best indication. *Inner strength* is probably a good description here and this may have been gained through the experience of personal suffering, so there is perhaps an element of the traditional meaning still relevant.

As a married person, she would have an independent streak and seemingly not need to rely on her partner to feel emotionally fulfilled or taken care of. She is happy and contented in her own right, capable of taking care of her own affairs and not emotionally needy. The Queen of Swords is simply a strong and independent woman.

She is very supportive and, so long as she's on your side (and believes you're in the right), she is a source of strength and will defend you boldly. This queen isn't afraid to speak her mind and there is usually a ring of truth to what she has to say, which can be unnerving for those not ready to hear it!

She is extremely well organized and efficient, an excellent champion for just causes or organizations that require a certain toughness to support them. Her work may be a good indicator of this and somewhere she may find release for that expression—areas of the law, for instance, but also in caring environments in which a strong leader that others can rely upon is required, such as a head teacher, a matron, or even top executive positions in which a woman must have strength to hold her own. A fast thinker, her analytical mind finds her happy anywhere that challenges her keen mind or wit.

The Queen of Swords on a most basic level can be a person of sharp words, but she can also be the "people's champion."

In the negative, she may be overly critical, intolerant, and have the ability to cut people to shreds with her words. Betray her and you won't get a second chance—she's not someone to pick an argument with!

Queen of Pentacles

QUEEN OF PENTACLES

This queen is usually materially secure. By nature, she tends to be warm, generous, practical, money-conscious, and often successful at anything she undertakes—including juggling a career and home. She is not afraid of hard work and would work methodically and tirelessly in order to succeed; as a result, she lives comfortably. A good businesswoman in her own right, she can also be found at the top of organizations. She works solidly and recognizes the virtues of doing things correctly. She makes good business decisions and is practically minded.

Note the peacock in this card; peacocks are usually regarded as a symbol of prosperity.

In her different guises, you would find the Queen of Pentacles as a wealthy woman—pleasant and generous to others. She carries off her role well. Wives of nobility, carrying titles, are frequently found running large estates and making them pay. Socially poised and correct in their manner, their clothing shows quality but rarely lacks the practicality of its purpose. These women work tirelessly and solidly, running households and businesses equally well.

They can also be found as independent career women, working steadily with their goals in sight, up the corporate ladder. Their success is always well deserved, as they're prepared to go the "extra mile" in order to achieve their objectives—and, unlike the Queen of Wands, the Queen of Pentacles will take care of the details, which is why she usually gets further in the long run.

On a different level, you may find these women working in finance: banks, accountancy, and so on; however, it is her characteristics that give her away—she never considers her work role as "just a job," but she does appreciate steadfastness, method, and routine.

These queens can be found as businesswomen, heads of organizations, or in anything connected to the earth element: property sales, accountancy, food services, jewelers, veterinarians, or in any form of agriculture or environmental issues. Farmers' wives usually fall into this category, too.

In the negative, they *may* be stubborn, liking things done their own way, and prone to jealousy. They can also be self-indulgent, and practical to the point of seeming dull or overly materialistic. Alternatively, due to their generous nature, others may take advantage of them.

The Minor Arcana—The Kings

The kings, although male, are similar to the queens in some respects, but show the more masculine side of their element—so, although you may find some similarities, you will also note subtle differences.

King of Wands

The king in this card is focused upon the fire that tops his wand. His throne appears to be set in the sky, perhaps an indication of how he is influenced by his many creative ideas.

The King of Wands is usually strong, optimistic, energetic, confident, and friendly by nature, good with words or motivating others, and quite physical. He enjoys challenges—so he is frequently found in leadership roles. They usually make good husbands, enthusiastic lovers, and proud fathers, although they tend to "talk up" their loved ones and can appear a bit showy to others.

These men are often found as entrepreneurs because they are always full of creative ideas and enthusiasm for their projects. They can, however, appear somewhat rash or impulsive in their decision-making, because they're not afraid to take risks.

In whatever role you find them, they stand out for their dynamic ways, and they like to feel a sense of freedom in being able to go about their work without restraint. Due to their high level of energy, they can be found in sport environments. They can also be found in sales positions or field sales, where they are left to their own devices, so long as they perform—but anywhere they can channel their apparently endless energy without restraint.

They like variety and get bored easily; as such, they dislike detail, which they feel bogs them down. They're good at delegating these tasks to others; you'll rarely find them taking care of such things themselves. The King of Wands is happiest when creating, and he has good vision.

In the negative, they may be rash, quick-tempered or hot-tempered, selfish, impatient, controlling, over-confident to the point of arrogance, and they may have an inflated ego.

King of Cups

KING OF CUPS

This king's throne sits upon the water. He appears relaxed and contented, in a thoughtful pose as he focuses upon his cup.

The King of Cups has a warm, genuine, easy going nature. He is generally the sort of man everybody likes, and he seldom has enemies. He is loyal, kind, and is usually family-oriented. He's a good husband, a thoughtful lover, and an adoring parent.

However, he can appear emotionally detached at times, as he wrestles with his inner thoughts and emotions.

The King of Cups is frequently found in the "helping" professions: medical care, consultancy, the church, teaching, or government agencies that deal with social work.

In whatever setting you may find him, he can be easily recognized due to his care and concern for others, although this usually manifests through his choice of career. These kings are not generally ambitious by nature—although that doesn't mean that in the right setting they won't achieve high positions—but it is not ambition alone that drives them, more likely their "cause."

Similarly, due to the water element that rules them, they are often found in the arts, and also in fashion, design, hair stylists, and so forth, because they are more easily at home with the feminine aspect of the water element (emotions and creativity) than the other elements.

However, the negative side of this is that they *may* lack drive or backbone. They dislike conflict to the point of denial; they can exasperate others by their complete withdrawal, be manipulative by withholding, or be sulky, childish, or passive-aggressive.

King of Swords

KING OF SWORDS

The King of Swords' throne sits in his element of air. His sword is prominently displayed and he appears to be in deep thought.

The King of Swords has a cool, detached air, which makes him rather difficult to fathom—a case of "still waters run deep," which can make him intriguing. Usually he is strong, with an easy air of authority and a just nature. He is a rational man with analytical thinking who prefers logic to emotion and likes clear, set rules.

Emotionally, he can appear misleading—for although he tends not to make great shows of public emotion, as a partner he is strong and loyal to his loved ones and takes his responsibilities seriously.

This king is often found in uniform: as a police officer, in the military, in law or government enforcement agencies, or as a prison or security officer—in fact, in any area of the law or discipline.

In higher positions, these men are usually extremely articulate with a razor-sharp mind, and have the ability to think quickly and responsibly. They also do well in mathematics, scientific fields, in investigative work, or as engineers.

In his presence, you get the distinct feeling you are being evaluated, and he would tend not to discuss his personal life, sticking to the purpose of the meeting. The King of Swords is careful where he places his trust, but he makes an excellent friend who gives good advice . . . when asked.

In the negative, he may seem cold and impersonal and lack sensitivity to others' feelings—in the extreme, cruel and bullying, with an ability to completely switch off his emotions.

King of Pentacles

This king's throne sits solidly on the ground, representative of the earth element. The back of his throne is a large golden pentacle. He appears quite comfortable, at ease with himself and his position.

This king is usually financially successful, an excellent businessman, comfortable within himself and in his position in life.

He has strong character and is dependable and steadfast. If he becomes angry, it is short lived and he doesn't brood. These men make excellent husbands and fathers, as they are loyal and reliable, and see their role as being a good provider. Family and tradition are important to them.

The King of Pentacles is not afraid of hard work and will see a task through to completion. His patience will often help him in his acquisitions; where the King of Wands would lose interest and pursue another deal, the King of Pentacles will sit it out, knowing that in the end he will get what he wants.

He is usually generous but never stupid with his money. His material possessions are carefully purchased and cared for; he does not waste, nor does he buy hastily.

Due to the earth element, these kings are often found in property and/or land development, as property and land owners, as financiers, in accountancy, or as stockbrokers. They are also found as farmers, builders, or tradesmen—all practical, money-conscious, hardworking, "salt of the earth" types.

In the negative, they *may* be extremely stubborn, blunt to the point of exasperation, overly materialistic, or miserly.

The Major Arcana

The major arcana holds the wisdom for our spiritual journey and the key to our lessons as we travel through life, seeking to understand, learn, and gain knowledge from our experiences, in an attempt to achieve the wholeness and harmony of our inner and outer realities.

0: The Fool

The Fool is something of a conundrum, for all is not as it may first appear in this card.

The image of the Fool that Ciro Marchetti presents to us appears to portray a court jester. In colorful clothes, he entertains, dancing and juggling with seemingly careless abandon. Yet on closer examination we find an apparent contradiction. For in his hands he masterfully suspends all the signs of the zodiac in the air; none carelessly slip to the floor. At this very moment in time, every conceivable potentiality exists, the wisdom of the heavens captured and contained within each sign and planet represented. At the same time, he spins a hoop and baton around his ankle—playful perhaps, but foolish it would seem not. There is a sense of innocent wisdom to this card.

The card number of zero represents the very moment before creation: unexplored potential. It is the only unnumbered card in the deck. Yet zero is also the endless circle and cycle of life, without beginning or end—alpha and omega.

Interpretation:

When the Fool appears in a reading, it suggests that unexpected opportunities will suddenly appear that can bring welcome changes. You need to remain open, as it will involve the need to make a major choice, seemingly out of the blue.

There are moments in life when we need to take a leap of faith and travel along paths that are unknown to us, but we grow as a result of our experiences.

The Fool is like the child within us that sees with innocence, imagination, and wonder; this side of ourselves invariably becomes lost due to social conditioning as we mature. However, the Fool is a reminder to listen to the voice of our inner child that recalls the excitement of new adventures and stepping out into unknown territory.

The Fool is usually a welcome and exciting card in a reading. I have frequently found that most people it appears for feel ready for the changes it can bring.

The only real negative aspect of this card is that people are usually afraid of making choices, mainly because they fear they might make the "wrong" one. You need to appreciate the potential that exists with this card. Unless badly aspected, the Fool is usually a positive omen and not one to miss!

I: The Magician

The Magician looks directly at us with a concentrated gaze. Before him we see the four elements of the Tarot represented—the tools of his trade magically and mysteriously suspended in the air, which he has mastered through dedication and concentration of will.

A bright light emanates from above his head; he is the link between heaven and earth that brings forth the manifestation of matter.

We are aware that we are in the presence of a Master, with fine-tuned abilities and skill.

The number one represents creative potential and power—the beginning.

Interpretation:

The Magician's message is to inform you that you have all the skills and ability required to handle a task well and bring it to a successful conclusion. Just like the Magician, you must apply yourself with concentration and willpower in order to succeed but you have all the potential to do so.

This is a time for action and initiative in any new ventures. You need to have confidence that you are indeed heading in the right direction.

THE HIGH PRIESTESS

II: The High Priestess

The High Priestess moves between two pillars, symbolizing duality. The crescent moon behind her and the glittering stars that adorn her head show her ability to access higher knowledge in esoteric matters. Her face is masked, representing mystery and secrets.

Draped in a transparent veil, she appears to be in a trancelike state. Engaged in the cosmic dance, she pays no heed to our presence nor our opinions. She seems secure within her own knowledge of universal matters.

She appears to defy natural laws as she floats above the water, which represents the subconscious and the world of the psyche.

To see as she does, first we must acquire her wisdom.

The colors of this card are muted and in varying shades of blue, relating to the moon and water, both symbols of the subconscious, imagination, and creativity.

Number two represents the duality of opposing forces, potential recognized but not yet expressed.

Interpretation:

The High Priestess represents mysteries and secrets, and so indicates that there is more depth to some matter than you have seen so far. With the right cards, it could show a secret becoming known to you that would be to your benefit. At this time, you need to follow your intuition and trust your instincts.

The High Priestess also carries the message of potential as yet unexplored, or perhaps unfulfilled; look at the situation again, as you may have missed something previously.

The influence of the card is feminine in nature, relating to the psyche, and so represents spirituality and esoteric matters, wisdom, and the desire for knowledge and learning. It may also show an interest in the deeper, more complex aspects of life.

III: The Empress

THE EMPRESS

The first and overriding impression from the Empress card is the care with which she holds the female symbol of Venus in her hands and the loving expression on her face toward it. The Empress is the representation of the female archetype in the Tarot, the desirable female form but also the loving, nurturing mother.

She is encircled by the signs of the zodiac, which, together with the symbol of the female, shows her ability to manifest life through the birthing process.

The colors of all four elements are represented here. Her red hair and flowing belt show the passion of fire, warmth, and nurturing; her gold dress symbolizes the love and emotion of water. Yet she is cloaked in green, representational of the earth element—the physical aspect of our being. She is shown against a backdrop of the sky, symbolizing the air element.

The combination of earthly and heavenly symbols represents the integration of spiritual and earthly matters, realizing the full potential of the two, therefore creating the third energy.

Interpretation:

The Empress represents growth, prosperity, and fertility. She brings happy conclusions to matters and promises good rewards for work and efforts. The Empress brings situations to fruition.

This is a card of nurturing, in all its forms, turning to potential fulfilled. This can be in creative and work endeavors but also with children and the family.

The Empress can represent pregnancy, birth, or motherhood, solid and happy relationships, and marriage. Accompanying cards will provide support.

She may sometimes represent a mother figure, although, as with all the majors, this card is usually symbolic of qualities, as opposed to a specific person—consider that to be the job of the court cards.

This is a wonderfully positive card, always well received by those seeking advice in relationships or fertility matters.

IV: The Emperor

THE EMPEROR

As the Empress represents the archetypal female, so the Emperor represents her masculine counterpart.

As befitting his title, we find before us a regal-looking character. His head is crowned with laurel leaves, representing triumph and success. He is suitably attired in rich and opulent gowns covered with symbols of the sun: a masculine sign, even to the clasp that holds his cloak of red—representing fire, which is again a male element. Even the stones he wears are rubies, a further representation of the sun. His robes and adornments symbolize the status of his position and his material success.

Behind him we see the signs of the zodiac displayed, but this time they have progressed to the more earthly representations they are known by. His scepter, topped with what appears to be the planetary solar system, points to earth and heaven. The hand that holds the top of the scepter reveals his index finger pointing to the heavens, to receive wisdom, and his other hand shows his index finger pointing to the earth where he uses that power; this also shows the need for rational thought with which to rule his subjects.

With so many masculine symbols, everything here suggests a powerful and dynamic man in control of the situation.

The number four represents stability, logic, and reason.

Interpretation:

When the Emperor appears in a reading, it is a sign of financial stability, ambition, authority, and also achievement. You need to keep a calm head at this time, make decisions based on facts, and not be overly influenced by your emotions.

This is a powerful card and a wonderful omen for business and career matters, as it shows great progress. Well placed, this card suggests you are in a powerful position to achieve your goals.

In relationships, it can also remind us to look at the situation in a more rational manner and not to become overly emotional regarding issues—to look at things with a clear head, in order to achieve successful results and financial stability for the family.

It can also represent a powerful male influence.

V: The Hierophant

The Hierophant is dressed in religious attire; his arms are open, showing his willingness to reveal his knowledge.

A beautiful stained-glass window stands between the moon, symbol of heavenly meditation, and the Hierophant, which represents the filter through which he receives his information. One hand is raised to heaven and the other faces down to earth, representing spirit and matter, with the Hierophant as the bridge between the two.

As the Emperor connects to material and worldly matters, the Hierophant represents the spiritual aspect.

Interpretation:

The Hierophant may indicate help from a wise, trusted person such as a mentor, teacher, or religious figure, usually one who is respected in the local community, but certainly someone whom the client holds in trust and high regard.

This card frequently refers to large institutions, such as hospitals, educational establishments, government offices, churches, or large organizations. It also suggests conformity and conventional, set ways of working or thinking, where it is difficult to implement change.

It can be representative of following traditional values and moral ethics, or the need to find a deeper meaning to life in the exploration of spiritual matters.

VI: The Lovers

THE LOVERS

The Lovers are shown as an idealized vision of romantic bliss. The perfect male and female forms are surrounded by water, symbolic of the world of our emotions. The potentiality of their sexual nature and blissful state in their togetherness are open and clear to see. From the heavens, they are touched by a golden aura of love that surrounds them.

The colors of this card combine indigo and mauve, indicative of the spiritual realm, and the fiery, passionate colors of red, orange, and gold.

Interpretation:

The image of this card portrays far more than mere words could hope to convey. Simply speaking, it represents human love and relationships. Here we have the harmony of the combined polarities, male and female, the perfect union expressed through love.

For me, the artwork of this card finally portrays the Lovers in the actuality that our human condition naturally desires. In older versions of this card, the Lovers often depicted three people and indicated choices, with the possible reference to the temptation of a third party—perhaps for this reason it has often been a common area of misinterpretation.

Yet, with regard to choice, the area of love relationships is perhaps one of the biggest arenas in which we experience personal growth and challenges, as we seek to harmonize self with another. As such, our relationships represent choices all the way through; this could be the choice of becoming involved in a new romance, or choosing to make a commitment in an existing relationship, such as marriage, or in a solid relationship making choices that will affect both partners.

The Lovers is a positive card, unless badly aspected, and surrounding cards will clarify what situation is being faced.

VII: The Chariot

A woman rides upon a chariot fronted by two sphinxes of opposite color, symbolizing opposing forces. She is dressed in opulent clothing and a large symbol of the sun, a powerful omen that rests above her.

And yet we see no movement—the Chariot in its current state is going nowhere! Where are the reins to steer this vehicle? The woman appears preoccupied, glancing to the side instead of focusing upon the road ahead.

There is a great deal of potential shown in this card, but the end result depends upon the effort expended to make it a reality.

Interpretation:

The Chariot is a card of triumph, though not without effort. It informs you that self-discipline will be required, but if you can master this then victory can be achieved. It signifies the qualities required to succeed over any obstacles that lie ahead. Self-discipline is a key word here, together with focus and perseverance.

This card tends to show an inner conflict (rather than external) that needs to be controlled in order to achieve success. Therefore, focus is needed upon one path; scattered energies will not bring achievement of the goal.

The Chariot can also indicate travel.

VIII: Strength

A beautiful maiden, her head bedecked in jewels, wears an expression of grace and purpose as she strides forward. She represents a pure expression of our female qualities.

The lion is considered to be the king of the jungle and a potent symbol of male energy, yet the gentle maiden appears to have him tamed. He walks beside her, held merely by a loose chain around his neck, which she handles lightly. It would appear that she has subdued the lion, not with brute force but with gentleness.

The lion is an expression of our inner strength, but controlled and manifested with the more gentle, feminine qualities of our nature.

Interpretation:

Feminine qualities such as patience and diplomacy (as opposed to aggression), combined with courage, will achieve the required results and bring success.

The Strength card reveals that you have a reserve of inner strength that provides you with more power than you realize. This can be expressed through quiet determination.

This card can also symbolize feminine charms to which men succumb, so it is particularly strong in a woman's reading regarding relationships.

IX: The Hermit

The Hermit stands on a solitary path. Dressed in a simple, plain robe, he carries only his staff to support him and a lantern that illuminates his way.

He is depicted as an elderly man with white hair and beard, representing the wisdom of his years. His expression is one of peace; he is comfortable in his solitude and his quest for inner knowledge.

Interpretation:

The Hermit signifies careful thought and contemplation, withdrawal from the outside world in order to reflect and find inner wisdom.

This card indicates that you have all the answers that you need within yourself, but perhaps you need some introspection to access them.

WHEEL OF FORTUNE

X: The Wheel of Fortune

The Wheel of Fortune sits against a backdrop of the heavens and planets; upon its face are shown the signs of the zodiac.

There is no human element shown here to influence the movement of the Wheel, so we are left to consider that fate is at work.

The movement of the Wheel depends upon the mechanics that drive it, and where it lands is a question of chance.

The Wheel represents the cycles of life, showing the transient nature of change.

Interpretation:

The Wheel of Fortune is also known as a "destiny" card. It brings a positive change of fortune unless badly aspected, and can indicate the commencement of a new cycle when progress can be made.

It is important to make the most of this fortunate time—for, as with anything, change is always just around the corner.

XI: Justice

The woman representing Justice stands between two pillars, signifying the need to balance duality. She wears white, representing the purity of her purpose, and she is blindfolded, signifying her impartiality. Before her stands the scales of justice, carefully balanced.

She holds her hands up to heaven and they are illuminated with a light that strikes down toward the symbol of the sun (male energy) that sits at the stem of the scales. The scales is a female symbol (the astrological sign of Libra) showing the need for balance.

The woman stands between a set of stone steps, perhaps representing our path so far; now is the time to make balanced decisions that will affect where our path leads us in the future.

The symbols throughout this card show the essence of duality through the two different energies represented, male and female (yin-yang), and the need to keep all things in balance—such is the nature of the universe.

Interpretation:

Justice is very much a card of balance, though more of the rational, logical kind, using the intellectual mind rather than the emotional self. A balanced mind will be required in order to come to a well-balanced decision that is fair and reasonable for all concerned.

It can represent the legal ruling upon a matter falling in favor of the rightful side. Legal documents are implied, including marriage agreements. Justice usually has a beneficial outcome, unless other cards indicate otherwise.

XII: The Hanging Man

A man hangs suspended by one leg, his other at an angle to his knee in a triangular fashion. His expression is one of peace and calm; he does not show suffering or anguish. We can see that this man could easily release himself from the chains around his ankle, were he so inclined, so his position appears to be by choice.

This card is often likened to the story of the god Odin, who hung himself from the Tree of Life for nine days and as a result achieved enlightenment. In many different cultures (including Native American cultures and the Eastern religions), it was commonplace for people to voluntarily place themselves in a difficult situation, fasting or undergoing some form of physical deprivation in order to achieve deeper spiritual awareness and enlightenment.

Interpretation:

Life may seem to be in a period of suspension, but this offers the opportunity to look at matters from a different and fresh perspective, which will bring a possible solution through better understanding.

This card can indicate self-sacrifice—sometimes we need to let go of something in the shorter term to gain something considered far more beneficial in the longer term. It can represent delayed gratification, which is also a form of self-sacrifice.

The Hanging Man card, despite its appearance, is not one to be feared; remember, the figure is in a voluntary position.

XIII: Death

Death represents only one part of the cycle of life and the image is a symbolic one—not literal! Since the image and title of this card is frequently misunderstood and therefore often feared, it is important to emphasize this from the outset.

A skeleton wearing black armor confronts us amid swirling banners of purple, a spiritual color. The black banner before Death displays the white rose, symbolic of purity; his shield bears a white horse, often associated with strength and the freedom of spirit.

Interpretation:

The Death card heralds the ending of one phase of life to make way for a new one. It represents major change and transformation.

To benefit from change, we need to remain open to it and recognize that through every life experience we have been given the opportunity for major growth and learning, on some level.

The Death card can release us from that which is no longer useful in our lives but that we continue to hang on to, merely because we fear change. In doing so, we deny ourselves new opportunities that await us.

Care is always needed when interpreting this card, as its image can be quite frightening. But when explained correctly, clients often welcome this card, for they may be impatiently waiting for major changes to take place. Surrounding cards will clarify the situation.

XIV: Temperance

A heavenly figure shrouded in stars carefully pours water from a golden cup of fire to a silver cup of water. Here we have the integration of opposites; silver represents the subconscious and gold the conscious—fire and water also being opposite elements. It shows the constant flow and balance necessary to attain harmony.

Sometimes referred to as the Alchemist, this card shows opposites being blended successfully.

Interpretation:

Temperance represents moderation, having patience, the ability to compromise to find satisfactory solutions, diplomacy and cooperation, and balanced emotions. It is a card of successfully integrating opposite forces.

With harmony and compatibility, it suggests the perfect union. It can also represent a receptive environment for reconciliation to take place.

Where Justice represents balanced thought, Temperance stands for balanced emotions.

Always a lovely, gentle card when it appears in readings, the Temperance angel often brings healing.

XV: The Devil

THE DEVIL

The Devil is an interesting card that has different connotations and, like most cards, can have positive and negative interpretations.

A masculine form engulfed in flames wears a horned mask (a further male symbol). The mask represents mystery, secrecy, but also possibly blindness. The pentacles behind him and on the mask represent the earthly element of our physical being.

Interpretation:

The Devil's presence quite often appears when a situation is dragging you down and you feel helpless to change it. It can show a form of "enslavement," whether to an ideal or an addiction, or even a manipulative or controlling relationship.

Overindulgence tends to result in upset, greed, or lust that can become self-destructive—overspending is a typical example. However, the important message is that it is *self*-enslavement; by taking control of this behavior, we are released from it and are free to walk away.

It can also carry an aspect of secrecy, such as secret plans being made, either by yourself or others around you. The surrounding cards would indicate which.

Let us not forget that, prior to being symbolized as an evil figure in religion, the Devil was previously identified as the pagan god, Pan.

Pan represents primal masculine energy at its most uninhibited level—procreative, sexual, untamed natural instincts that represent the very nature of life itself. Thus, this card can show a healthy (or improving) sex life—strong and impulsive urges, lust for life, and so on. But taken to extremes, this behavior can become obsessive or addictive.

It can indicate a passionate or compelling relationship, with a strong physical attraction—although it does not necessarily imply a healthy one. Surrounding cards will verify.

XVI: The Tower

A large, sturdy tower is hit by lightning, flames billowing out from within the structure. A man plunges headlong into the unknown. His naked state perhaps indicates that all he carries with him is his knowledge; at this moment, material possessions are of little use.

The Tower represents "man-made" beliefs and philosophies, frequently false, and the lightning from heaven the moment of illumination, to see things as they really are. "The truth shall set you free."

Interpretation:

A house that has been built without good foundations must collapse, sooner or later. The Tower represents such situations, for anything that has been built on illusion or false beliefs is now coming to an end. In the positive, it means having the ability to see the truth in a matter and to build anew for the future—this time with solid foundations.

This is never an easy card when it appears in a reading because it shows a sudden or unexpected ending that *may* bring a sense of catastrophe or chaos with it. This can be in regards to situations that have been relied upon as being permanent and can relate to any area of life.

This card is not always totally unexpected; sometimes when the Tower is drawn, there is already anticipation of something of this nature—yet often people will try to stay blind to the possibility, having a sense of denial. But this is not always the case, as the Tower tends to indicate something collapsing that was falsely believed to be true—so please treat this card delicately.

It is helpful to recognize how the Tower fits into your life (other cards in the reading should help you see this), what preparations you can make in readiness, and how you can improve matters afterward. There is always something positive that can be done.

XVII: The Star

A bright star illuminates a young woman as she pours water from her two pitchers. The pitchers are gold, representing the conscious, while the water represents the subconscious. The woman brings renewal, as water is life-giving. She provides harmony and balance to both the physical and the emotional plane.

She sits within the pool of water, representing the emotions, but we can see from the star on her forehead that her thoughts are illuminated. Her naked state represents truth.

Traditionally, stars are a good omen representing hope, peace, and faith. From the night sky, stars can be used to find our way home, so they are seen as a helpful guide on our pathways through life.

Interpretation:

The Star is the card of hope; it brings a sense of optimism and tells us to have faith, safe in the knowledge that better times are ahead of us.

The Star can bring healing after illness. Its beautiful aspect means it is *always* a welcome sight in any situation. It provides faith and tells us to have belief in our self. Our plans show promise; success is attainable by the light of the Star.

In relationships, it can show the healing of rifts, harmonious living conditions, and hope for the future. A new relationship aspected with this card would tend to show shared harmony and a good future.

For those who have been hurt in love, the Star provides the confidence to leave the past behind and find love again, knowing that better things are destined.

THE MOON

XVIII: The Moon

The moon dimly lights the scene below. Dogs howl at the moon and a crayfish rises from the water, representing the subconscious world. There is a sense of mystery to the entire scene.

The moon has long been recognized for the effects it has on all life forms. Its gravitational pull upon the earth controls the tides; fish spawn at the time of the full moon. As our bodies contain a large proportion of water, we also experience the same kind of magnetic pull that the moon has upon the earth.

Crime levels and births increase at the time of the full moon, with emotions and tempers running higher than usual. So there is much to be said for "moon madness."

Interpretation:

The Moon represents illusionary situations, possible deceptions, and feelings of uncertainty. Emotions are highly charged and fluctuating, like a pendulum swinging back and forth.

Due to the mystical associations of the Moon, it can also show our dreams becoming more vivid as the subconscious reveals itself to us. Feelings of intuition and gut instincts are heightened.

When this card is present, it also warns that it's important not to jump to conclusions, for the light of the moon can create illusions, shapes in the shadows that are not what they seem. There is usually far more to a situation than first meets the eye and it would be wise to be watchful but not to act in haste, taking time until the situation has revealed itself more clearly.

XIX: The Sun

The sun is depicted as the central body in the cosmic scheme. The journey of the planets as they map across the heavens, with everything in its rightful place, is charted in relation to the signs of the zodiac.

The sun is a male, active energy of the conscious mind and physical plane. It provides us with warmth, energy, and daylight. The sun's light illuminates everything clearly and all of life responds to its warmth.

Interpretation:

The Sun is one of the most positive cards in the Tarot, for it brings happiness, success and triumphs, excellent relationships, a happy marriage, contentment, prosperity, and good health.

The Sun tends to shine favorably upon any situation. When this card is present, it is important to make the most of its favorable aspects.

XX: Judgement

A winged messenger in the heavens heralds liberation with a blazing trumpet and brings resurrection to the men and women rising toward it.

The card signifies Judgment Day and represents karma.

Interpretation:

Judgement is known as the karmic card: "as you sow, so shall you reap."

The results of the seeds you have previously planted, and your past efforts, are now being rewarded.

As a card depicting resurrection, it indicates renewal and revival, dormant matters coming back to life. With the Judgement card, it is possible to make a new start, but it is important to take stock before positively moving forward again.

There is a general feeling of rejuvenation, and health matters show improvement.

This card represents a time to be happy, with new beginnings afoot.

XXI: The World

THE WORLD

A female dancer wearing purple (the color of spirituality and wisdom) stands in a confident pose. In each hand she holds a white wand, representing polarization and the unity of duality, which has been a theme throughout the major arcana. This represents the final synthesis of combining and harmonizing two opposites into one.

She stands upon a golden light, surrounded by a wreath of laurel leaves, representing victory and triumph, against a backdrop of the world, the moon, and the stars, representing our universe in its state of perfection.

The images represent the perfect union of all things, oneness with the cosmos, self-realization, the harmonizing of all states— inner and outer, self and nature—and the return to the original divine state from which we came, to which we are now returned, our rightful place in the cosmos. It is the perfected state to which seekers of enlightenment, of all different religions, aspire.

Interpretation:

Having learned the lessons presented by all the previous cards in the major arcana, we finally arrive at the World.

The World brings the assurance of success, victory, and triumph. This card doesn't indicate overnight success, but rather the accomplishment of a goal that has been steadily worked toward; rewards are well deserved and you will feel delighted with your achievements.

Success, attainment, confidence, happiness, a sense of completion, and fulfilment are all indicated.

With supporting cards, the World may also represent traveling or a new home that brings happiness.

Preparation
for Readings

Part Three

STEP 16

Getting Ready to Read

By now, you should have completed your Tarot diary for each card, complete with any past or present experiences from your own life, or that of others, that you can relate to any of the cards.

Before you start to do readings for yourself, you will need to shuffle your deck as much as possible, in preparation. I also recommend sleeping with the cards under your pillow once more. The intention now is to do some spreads for yourself and record them, so you can check the accuracy of your readings before you begin reading for others.

In the explanations that follow, you will find references to reading for others and various guidelines included, as at some point you will be ready to do such readings.

Reading for yourself

The most important thing about self-readings is that you need to be objective. One of the biggest mistakes that people make with self-readings is that they repeatedly lay out the cards, time after time, trying to get the answers they want. Or, they don't like the look of the cards, so they do it all again. This will never give you accurate readings.

It is important that you follow the same procedures as if you were the client, with the same care of preparation. After all, if you were going to a professional reader, he or she wouldn't perform one spread after another for you on the same question.

Preparation

Ensure that you will not be disturbed and allow enough time to do your reading properly. You need quiet so you can focus, and you don't want constant interruptions from the telephone, people walking in and out, and so on, as it will break your concentration.

Lay your cloth on the table before you and repeat the protection process detailed earlier before shuffling your cards. Take a few moments to relax, and consider what question you would most like guidance on at this time.

Asking the Tarot

It helps your focus if you formulate your question on paper to begin with, then speak it aloud—so you can ask your question with clarity and without a hundred other thoughts interrupting. Once you have asked your question, let it go, in the safe knowledge that it has been heard. There is such a thing as "trying too hard," so allow your mind to be as relaxed as possible, without focusing upon what you think or hope the cards will say.

It is important to phrase your question as clearly as possible, as this will help you to achieve the clearest answer. Ensure that it is only one question and not a sentence containing more questions, as you could be confused by the response.

Some people recommend that you don't ask "yes-no" questions, but I think—so long as you realize that the Tarot doesn't answer in the same fashion—that it's absolutely fine. For instance, you could ask if your financial situation will improve; clearly, we have seen there isn't a card that just says yes or no. However, the responses received will give a clear indication of what to expect. This is an area I feel that people can labor upon unnecessarily; a question is a question and the Tarot will respond. Just don't be ambiguous in the way you ask it.

Here are some examples of how you might consider phrasing your questions:

"What will happen if I...?"
"Please advise me on my current career prospects with..."
"What will happen if I proceed with...?"
"What is the future potentiality of...?"
"Will I successfully...?"
"What will be the outcome of...?"
"How will my relationship progress with...?"
"What is the likely outcome of...?"

Please don't ask your question of the cards repeatedly; you need time to consider their response and for events to unfold. If you ask the same question three times in one night, or the same question every night, then how are you going to assess the cards' responses and accuracy?

If you do not have a specific question, then you can always ask the cards, "What do I most need to be aware of at the moment? Please provide me with your guidance and wisdom." Unless you have a pressing need for an answer in a specific area, this is always an excellent question. When reading for myself, I always find this is a good starting point.

Shuffling and cutting

Please don't shuffle the Tarot at a hundred miles an hour, or in an agitated fashion; this agitation will be passed on to your cards. Shuffle calmly and ask your question as clearly as possible. From here you do not need to focus upon the situation you ask about—in fact, it is better if you do not. This may seem contradictory, as most accounts suggest concentrating upon your question; however, it allows the mind to get out of its own way. I have found that once the cards are consulted, they don't need to be reminded of the task at hand! It is far better when the questioner is relaxed than focused intensely upon the question. Take your time, as it is important to create the link and for your answer to be formulated. There will come a moment when the cards feel "right," and this is when you stop.

As already mentioned, please don't use any fancy shuffling methods; simply shuffle one over another in the normal fashion, using both hands.

Some readers don't like anyone to touch their cards and only allow the client to choose from a spread fan, once they have shuffled the cards themselves. However, I feel it is important to allow the client's energy to mingle with the cards (when the client is present). I always tell people to take their time and not to worry if the cards feel awkward, but to give them a really good shuffle.

Always pay attention to any cards that seem to "leap" out of the deck during the shuffling process—they can be very insightful, as if demanding to be seen and heard.

Take the pile of cards, face down, and hold them just slightly above the table surface. Allow them to slip through your fingers into three piles to the left, as follows:

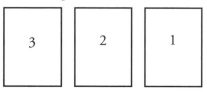

So, pile number one will have come from the very bottom of the stack; then number two next to the left of number one; and then put down the last pile in your hands to the left again, to make number three.

Collect the cards back into one pile beginning with pile number one first, then two underneath, and then three, so the cards from stack one are now at the top.

Now the cards are ready to lay out.

It is perhaps worth pointing out at this stage that you should keep the deck you use for your own readings separate from the cards you use for others, so a second deck is worth purchasing once you begin to read for others.

Ensure that you thoroughly "cleanse" the deck in between readings for different people to clear the previous energy. Cut the deck in the usual way, shuffle the cards well, and then repeat the process again, finishing with a final cut. By doing so, I feel it underlines the fact that the reading for that particular client has been completed and thoroughly mixes the cards. I like to verbalize the process in my mind, too, thanking the cards for their guidance and asking that they now be cleansed of the previous client's energy.

Using a significator

A significator refers to a Tarot card that is selected to represent the client; this card is taken from the deck and laid down, prior to the reading.

I don't use this format. I think it is more informative to see if a card representing the client appears in the reading, which can provide valuable information. Neither would I take a card to represent someone else the client knows, with the view of doing a reading about this person. I don't feel this is ethical practice without the person's consent; it's like invading someone else's privacy and it is debatable whether the information, used in this way, can be classed as accurate.

However, if a court card appears in the client's reading and more information is required, as to how or why this person would be influential to the client's future, then I would take the card from the reading and use it to do a continuation, usually with the Celtic Cross Spread. In this case, the client would then specifically ask the relevant question pertaining to this person in his or her reading. This card would be in the first position with the layout placed over the top. So the first card dealt would show what covers the situation with this person, what crosses the situation, and so on. As such, this can be very useful.

If the client has a particular question that involves other people, then you can help him or her to identify which court cards represent these people before doing the reading, so there's no confusion once the cards appear. But this tends to be more useful when a number of people are involved in a situation, not just one. However, I have found that when a court card appears in a reading, the client normally identifies the person fairly quickly anyway, using the normal interpretations.

It is worth mentioning that one should always use the court cards and never a major arcana card as a significator.

Recording readings in your diary

As you start to do spreads for yourself and ask questions, you should record these questions in your diary. For privacy reasons, please ensure that the only readings you record in your diary are your own.

The format I use is quite straightforward and fairly quick once you become accustomed to it. Lined paper comes in useful here, as a guide for lots of little box drawings, representing the cards drawn. I use drawings for the elements, such as the letter I for wands, a simple goblet for cups, a pentacle, and a cross for swords—none of which are very artistic, just shorthand that I understand. I find it works extremely well to draw out the spread, rather than just making numbered listings. Again, you will find that once you are familiar with the cards, the images immediately present themselves in your mind's eye, so drawing out the spread is like actually looking at it.

Underneath, or on the next page if you prefer, interpret the cards in the positions drawn and finish with a summary of what you feel is the answer or guidance given. This may seem very long and drawn out, but I can guarantee that if you don't make a note, two or three spreads (or days) later, the precise reading will be hazy.

By taking the time to record your readings, you will often find far more depth than when you first looked upon it. So this method is not only an extremely good way to reinforce your learning, but it also disciplines you not to be too dismissive of what you first see.

It is quite amazing to look back over your diary, review the questions you asked, and see how things turned out. Going back and making notes of this underneath the original reading is the key element to fine-tuning your experience.

Example of Tarot diary record

Date and time:
Question:

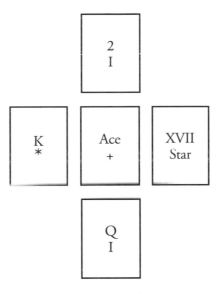

(1) Present—Queen of Wands (your interpretation of the card in this position follows)
(2) Desires—Ace of Swords (as above)
(3) Helpful matters—The Star
(4) Challenges—King of Pentacles
(5) Outcome—Two of Wands

Summarize your interpretation:

(Also, leave a space to come back later and record what happened.)

Take the time to go back and study the reading later; make a note of the timing, too, as this provides you with a general idea of how long events took to materialize. Your personal experience will provide the key and you will find it very accurate when you are helping others later.

Before you begin, some helpful advice

- Once you have laid the cards out, just stop for a moment before rushing to interpret them. Don't feel overwhelmed. Take a deep breath.
- What is your first reaction to the cards?
- Which elements are present? Are there more of one suit, or a predominance of courts, majors, or minors?
- Write all this down—first.

If there is a predominance of one suit, then the element of that suit immediately tells you something. Likewise, if there are a number of court cards, you can see there are many people involved. This may seem like a lot of details when all you want is the answer! But it will prepare you well for larger spreads in the future and it allows your subconscious to sift through the information while you keep your conscious thoughts busy.

Now, remove yourself from the situation and ask yourself honestly, "What would I say to someone else if this were their reading?" Then verbalize it, as though you were. Speaking out loud stops the clutter of thoughts clouding your mind and focuses your attention—it helps. Also, if you do feel you've gone "blank," simply verbalizing the imagery of the card will start your thoughts flowing, and you should find that the rest follows. Try it!

In your diary:

- Record the date and time of the reading
- Record the question asked
- Record the layout used
- Make a record of the cards using the relevant template provided at the end of this book
- Write down the interpretation of the cards in each position
- And finally, summarize what you believe the reading indicates.

You may wish to refer back to the meanings to begin with, but as you progress try not to become reliant on them. If you have used your diary correctly and followed the exercises for each card, then you actually have the information stored in your mind and your subconscious will bring it together.

It is usually a lack of confidence that will make you re-check, so try and work it out before you rush to look at the meanings. This way you may be pleasantly surprised with yourself! Also, you can then take note of which cards you felt you struggled with. You will discover that there are some cards you remember and associate with more easily than others, and this in itself can be quite telling, but don't beat yourself up over it.

Various Tarot
Spreads
in Depth

Part Four

What type, when, and why?

Beyond ethics, there are very few "rights" or "wrongs" with Tarot. With regard to spreads, it is a case of what you feel most comfortable with and what works best for you. This, as you may have gathered, is going to be a case of practice, trial, and error. Most people settle down to just a few spreads that they use regularly—it really is an area of personal choice.

A spread is designed to help you access information through the ordering of the cards, with different positions having set meanings, so it's simply a case of what you find best results with and enjoy using. In time, you may even decide to design some spreads of your own and that is also quite acceptable. It means considering what information you want from a spread and designing it accordingly. Then you would use it for yourself consistently, recording your results over a period of time, to see how it fares.

Most spreads follow a fairly similar theme, since there is certain information that is almost always useful to know (i.e., the current situation, what is hoped for, favorable conditions, challenges, and the outcome). In other situations, some history of the past circumstances can be helpful, so you will find a selection of differing types of spreads.

Don't be put off by the larger spreads. I have had beginners tell me how much easier they found them to work with, compared to smaller ones. I also found working with fewer cards more difficult, so for this reason I will avoid the often-found recommendation of beginning with only one or three cards.

With this said, the first layout for you to try is a simple design of my own. It contains five cards and is very good for providing clear guidance on a specific issue. You can't get lost in lots of background information, or feel flummoxed by too many cards—but don't underestimate it. This spread may not always be appropriate for certain questions, especially where background information would be beneficial, but it has its place. As you learn other spreads, you will come to use different ones, as appropriate, based on your experiences.

STEP 17

The Cross of Truth

Having shuffled and cut your cards as directed, take the cards, still face down, in your left hand (vice versa if left-handed) and with your dominant hand, take the cards from the top of the stack, one at a time, turning them over as you place them into position in an unhurried manner.

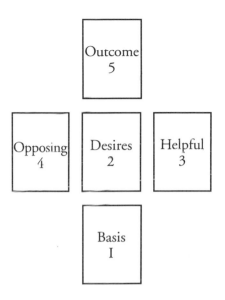

Card position #1—Basis or present

The first card shows your present position, the base from which you are working, in relation to your question.

Card position #2—Desires (hopes or fears)

The second card shows how you really feel about the situation. This in itself can tell a great deal about your mindset. How in tune is this card with the others? Is it in conflict or agreement with what you want and what the other cards say?

If this card is positive and the other cards are negative to the result you were hoping for, it could be that you're not in tune with the situation as it really is.

Card position #3—Helpful matters

This card shows what is (or will be) working in your favor in relation to your question.

Card position #4—Challenges (opposing energies)

The card in the position of challenges show if there are opposing energies preventing you from achieving what you are hoping for, or challenges you may face. Don't be misled if a positive card appears here; sometimes the circumstances surrounding the meaning of the card actually create an obstacle.

Card position #5—Outcome

The final card will provide the answer or advice you need, but always read it in relation to the other cards.

About your reading

Having asked this particular question, restrain yourself from asking it again today—and, unless circumstances have changed—tomorrow or the day after, either. At the risk of repeating myself, if you went to a professional, that would be your answer. You wouldn't call every day with the same question. It's important that you allow the answer time to materialize, in which case you would probably then have another question. But repeating the same question every day is not going to help and it certainly won't help you to record the accuracy of your readings. It would just become confusing.

Whether your answer is positive or negative, don't forget: it is the potentiality of the current situation, and your actions can change the outcome. Therefore, if your answer is positive, don't become over-confident, thinking no matter what you do you'll get the desired result! It is important to continue down the road you were traveling.

For example: you've recently had a quarrel with your partner, so your question was, will he contact you? The cards look very positive. The phone rings; confident it's all going to go your way, you decide to make him wait a bit longer and don't answer, thinking he'll call again. See what I mean? Previously, the chances are you would have picked up the phone the first time—or else why would you bother to ask the question to start with?

Since the layout will *not* give you a definite yes or no, it's important to follow the advice that the cards provide. They may show delays before a positive outcome, or tell you to be patient. The Tarot always offers good advice. And if you don't like the look of where things are heading, then take steps to change the route you were following, in order to change the outcome. In which case, you can also consult the Tarot to see which course of action would prove most beneficial. Remember . . .action shapes destiny!

What if the cards seem unrelated?

Sometimes when you ask a specific question of the cards, the answer appears to make little sense. If this is the case, I recommend recording and interpreting the answer anyway, in your diary. However, please check how you phrased the question. Was it clear enough? Can you reword it differently to be more concise? If so, go ahead and do the reading again, but please be aware that every card appears for a reason, so don't discount any of the cards.

Occasionally, you may ask the cards about one thing and they bring an entirely different situation to your attention. For instance, you may ask about work and instead find the whole reading appears to relate to your love life. In this instance, I advise you to read the cards as they are presented; don't try and make them fit the original question. There will be relevance as to why these cards appear; it must be important or else they wouldn't be there. Perhaps there is something more pressing in that particular area that the universe wishes to make you aware of at this time. You can always continue with your original question afterward.

Interestingly, I have found that if the cards are discounted, reshuffled, and the original question asked again, invariably the same cards reappear. Unbelievable as it may seem, sometimes these have been in precisely the same order, even though they were well shuffled! If you feel flummoxed as to why such cards should appear, then this would be a good time to ask the cards for their wisdom (as outlined above). Or, you can take one of the relevant cards and ask for more information. . . but we shall cover this in more detail further on.

Please remember that you are looking at a future situation. Something that may not seem relevant now may become so at a later date. It is a natural reaction to read the cards based on the facts we have to hand but, in reality, there are always many hidden factors at work, of which we are unaware.

The cards shown are always relevant—your job is to interpret them. Stay true to the meanings and look for the links between them. Again, I emphasize: what would you say to someone you don't know if you were reading for them? With self-readings, always let that question be your guide.

Checking your accuracy

Later, as situations come to pass, you can go back to the interpretation recorded in your diary and study it. Were you accurate? Now that you know the situation that came to pass, can you see what you missed, or misinterpreted?

This is very important to your learning process and is the experience you will draw upon later. Once you can see the accuracy of your readings for yourself, it will give you great confidence, both in your own ability and in the Tarot.

Sample reading: The Cross of Truth

This reading is based on a "Will he contact me?" type question. In this particular case, the card in the position of "challenges" appeared to be positive, but the client's situation brought further information to light, of which I was originally unaware. So the results were quite interesting and give a good example how the cards can relay information—a good reason to stay true to the interpretations, even if they appear unlikely to you at the time.

Card position #1—Basis/present position—Two of Swords
The present situation showed a stalemate; a deadlock appeared to be in place. The client, Carole, said she felt precisely as this card suggests. She had stated her position to her partner regarding their relationship and had not yet heard back from him. She felt there was nothing further she could do at this time, since she'd stated her position calmly but firmly and left the ball in his court. Much now rested on his response. Since she hadn't heard back from him, she felt "stuck" in the situation, not knowing where it was going.

Card position #2—Desires—Page of Pentacles
Carole was, of course, hoping for good news that would bring welcome changes. In addition, she was busying herself with a new learning project and, although she found it hard to concentrate because of her relationship problem, she was persevering with her studies. She knew, whichever way the relationship went, that it was important to focus on her own life and ambitions also (sensible woman!) She was also using the spare time she had to focus on activities with her son, a very academic child. (That doesn't always happen, but shows how sometimes all the different aspects of the card can be relevant.)

Card position #3—Helpful matters—Knight of Wands
The Knight of Wands indicated swift movement with a high degree of energy. It suggested travel—usually indicating a long journey, sometimes over water. It can also indicate a change of residence, which was quite puzzling since the card in position four was the Ten of Pentacles.

The reading suddenly became very interesting. Carole revealed that her partner was now living in another country and she had hoped they could sit down and discuss matters properly together, which would involve one of them making a long journey. She didn't know if the distance had become a total barrier to their relationship or if he felt seriously about her anymore, as he had previously indicated he had before he moved. So there might be a journey over water, if the invitation arrived.

Card position #4—Challenges—Ten of Pentacles

The Ten of Pentacles is the card of the home and family, tradition, and financial stability. Interestingly, when the Knight of Wands appears with the Ten of Pentacles, it usually indicates a change of residence. The Knight of Wands, as well as a journey, can indicate immigration. However, the ten was in the position of challenges. How did the family home represent a challenge?

Carole reported that since they both had their own homes in different countries, their livelihoods and children also came into the equation. She stated that if there were a move it would have to be from her end, and this is why there would be so much to consider. Her partner had a good position, so it wouldn't make a great deal of sense for him to move. So where they both lived, as individuals, now posed a problem to the relationship strengthening, and it would obviously have to be serious for her to move to be with him. Carole felt there was a great deal to consider and discuss if the relationship were to progress—hence, the original situation in card one becomes more apparent.

Card position #5—Outcome—Nine of Cups

This is the wish card, signifying the fulfillment of an important, desired wish and emotional fulfillment. This card shows a positive outcome and it appears to be good news.

In summary, all the indications are that Carole would hear from her partner and that a journey would be made so they could discuss their future. Although the Nine of Cups is a very positive card, it does not have the same stability as the Ten of Cups. Had this been the case, with the Knight of Wands and the Ten of Pentacles together, it could have shown a commitment to the relationship, ultimately moving and setting up home together or marriage. Although it still showed good possibility, I felt a little more cautious than I would have, had the Ten of Cups been in the outcome position.

However, Carole indicated from our conversation that she would not anticipate marriage or permanency just yet. Although the relationship appeared to hold a lot of potential, she didn't feel they had known each other long enough to make those kind of decisions just yet, and the distance had lengthened the whole process a bit more. However, the indications were good that the relationship would continue in order for them to explore the possibility of a future together.

Points to note

In this instance, the positive card in the challenges position was not an attitude problem or lack of belief from the client. Holding true to the card's meaning, however unlikely it may seem to you, is important, as this case indicated—since it made perfect sense once the client elaborated.

The Cross of Truth is actually a good place to start with your practice. The most popular spread that is normally recommended for beginners is the three card Past-Present-Future spread, but I feel this is a difficult way to begin. We also want to learn to link the cards in progression, as this is a very important part of readings frequently overlooked for beginners. To build upon this exercise, a better variation is to work with nine cards, which is our next spread.

The Nine-Card Spread

| 1 | 2 | 3 | | 4 | 5 | 6 | | 7 | 8 | 9 |

Past **Present** **Future**

Always use the same format:

- Formulate the question (write it down to help focus)
- Verbalize the question
- Shuffle the deck
- Cut the deck three times, as shown, then recollect into one pile
- Lay out the cards

Take a moment to get first impressions—don't go into blind panic at this moment! Ignore that little voice in your head saying you haven't got a clue what it all means; that's just lack of confidence. You *do* know or, more importantly, your subconscious does.

Take a deep breath and start to verbalize the first card, as if you were reading for someone else. I know I've said this before—but so often we read books and when they tell us to do something, we tend not to!

With the Nine-Card Spread, you are able to see more clearly how past events have influenced the present and ultimately the future outcome. Reading for yourself, you are also fully aware of past issues—once you see this link for yourself in your own readings, it will provide you with a great deal of confidence when reading for someone else when you wouldn't already know all the information. With this spread, you are given more background information.

Don't assume that the three cards in each position will appear to naturally follow on, or link to one another—sometimes they may appear disjointed, but in many cases the history of a situation is not just narrowed to one particular aspect. In a love question, for instance, if work and money cards came out, could it not be that a work aspect was involved in creating a problem, or that the relationship started at work, or through a contact at work, and so on?

Firstly, look to see if there is a link, a theme that blends the three. You may find there are two or three separate links that follow through in each section of Past and Present. There are no hard and fast rules here, as there are obviously differing combinations that can appear. The best way to become familiar with this spread is to use it for yourself and record the results in your diary.

However, don't feel as if you have to use it. If it doesn't feel comfortable for you, or you don't feel particularly happy with the results, then use a spread that you feel more comfortable with. There are plenty more to choose from. But it does provide a useful exercise in learning to link the cards.

The Celtic Cross

Personally, I think this is one of the most underestimated spreads around. For whatever reason, perhaps because it is so well known, some seem to consider it "old hat." Hmm . . . I think you may be surprised at the amount of information this spread can pull out of that old hat! So please don't dismiss the Celtic Cross.

We will look at this spread in finer detail due to the myriad of clues it gives, beyond what is immediately obvious. This spread is also the only one I have found to consistently deliver accurate results for timings. It is equally good for answering specific questions or asking for general guidance and wisdom, and therefore remains one of my firm favorites.

There are a number of variations to the Celtic Cross, but this is the version I use, with a small addition:

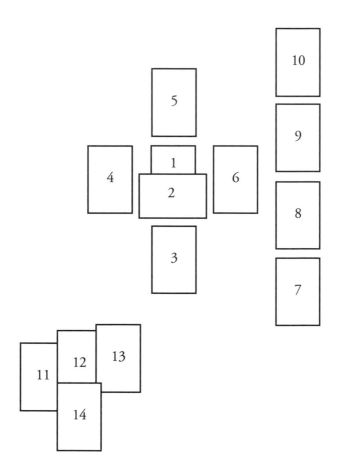

Card position #1—Present

"This is what covers you..."

This card tends to show the client's present position, what he or she is experiencing in relation to the question, or something currently affecting him or her.

Card position #2—Influence

"This is what crosses you..."

The crossing card works like a filter, so it shows whether the energies surrounding the situation are helpful or challenging in relation to the question. This is not a predictive card as such, and (as always) must be read in connection with the rest of the reading. But it does show what is working for or against the situation.

Card position #3—Past issues

"This is the basis of the situation..."

This card will provide more information regarding the past in relation to the question, and is often the reason, or foundation, of why the client is asking the question.

Card position #4—Immediate past

"This is behind you..."

This card shows the influences that have either just passed or are now passing through—if they haven't yet happened, allow a week or two for them to manifest.

Card position #5—Crowning thoughts

"This is what crowns you..."

The card in position five shows the client's "crowning" thoughts in relation to the question. As any esoteric practices or personal development material will tell you, our thoughts are very real. They go forward and manifest, so they have an enormous impact on how situations can inevitably turn out, based on our attitude toward what is happening, or as we believe it. Our attitude always has some bearing on the eventual manifestation and outcome. So guard your thoughts! Although this card is not actually in a predictive position it does show a strong possibility of how the situation could develop, based on the client's beliefs with regard to his or her question.

Card position #6—Immediate future
"This is before you…"

The card in position six shows what is about to happen in the immediate future. Since we must consider that this card has already been brought into being by the energies of the past and present, there is a greater likelihood of its manifestation.

Card position #7—Your fears
"These are your fears…"

The seventh card shows what apprehensions the client is experiencing emotionally in relation to their question. Don't be misled if a positive card shows here; it can show unfounded fears.

Card position #8—Environmental factors
"This is how others (will) view you…"

The eighth card allows the client to see how other people around them will be viewing the situation. If the question has been asked concerning one particular person then this card reveals their view—this can be an extremely insightful and helpful card!

Card position #9—Your hopes
"These are your hopes…"

This card shows what the client really hopes for in relation to their question.

Card position #10—Outcome

"This is the outcome…"

The final card of the Celtic Cross shows the outcome and answer to the question. However, it must be read in conjunction with all the other cards present. Don't just dash ahead to the last card.

Card positions 11, 12, 13, and 14—Reader's fan

These cards are placed as a fan, away from the main Celtic Cross. Please do not let this distract you from the main reading. The purpose of the fan is only to clarify the cards that are already present.

This is more for your own purpose so, as such, it has no particular aspect and can be a mixture of past, present, or future influences. While it can provide further information, it is not a continuation of the reading, as if it were read upward from the tenth card, so do not allow it to distract you. The interpretations should tie in with what you already see in the main ten cards. Since it is for your own guidance, you wouldn't necessarily read these cards to the client, but they can be very helpful to you in clarifying the reading. However, if you find it confusing, then leave this part out. Always using the Anchor (as covered shortly) and leaving it in place will help you to clarify all your second readings that follow.

Further insights from the Celtic Cross

Once you have laid the cards out before you, take a moment to assess if any particular suits and so on are prevalent, as covered previously. However, there are further insights to be gained from this reading.

Cards 5, 7, and 9—The client's attitude

Card #5—Crowning thoughts

Card #7—Your fears
Card #9—Your hopes

Take a moment to assess these cards; are they in tune with the rest of the reading? More specifically, are they in tune with the cards (6 and 10) that define the outcome? All these cards relate to the client's attitude. As we have already covered, this can have a significant effect on how events will unfold because how clients feel about something will affect their behavior and what actions they will take. It is possible to be either over- or under-confident and these cards will reveal whether the client is in balance with the situation. With this information, you can help clients enormously in their understanding and therefore help them to understand how they can successfully progress. Their fears can prevent exactly what they want, and this happens far more than you may realize.

For instance, let us say a client is considering setting up a new business and asks how successful it would be. The following is an extreme example, but it's intended to make a point. Let's imagine that in positions 5, 7, and 9, he has highly positive cards, such as the Nine of Cups, the Sun, and the World. Yet cards 6 and 10 don't show a very promising future—the Ten of Swords and the Tower. That is a typical example of someone being overly optimistic.

In addition, you could find further clues: position 1 could be the Ace of Wands, showing the client's enthusiasm for his new venture, but it could be crossed by the Five of Wands, showing that conflicts, opposition, or competition may be met. In position 8, the Five of Pentacles shows how others view the situation (it shows the client suffering material loss.)

Imagine the Three of Swords in position number 3 or 4. We discover he and his wife have quarreled and she doesn't want him to start the business. His wife not being supportive could present further opposing energies that he isn't considering.

This gives you some indication of the various clues that are available with this spread. Although the examples I have given may seem ridiculously obvious, I believe you will be surprised how clear the client's reading actually becomes to you, once you know what to look for.

Cards 3 and 7—Base and Fears

It is interesting how many times these two cards link and provide further information about what is going on around a client. To give an example:

A client's question was concerning business, and while the other cards reflected this, those in positions 3 and 7 were the Six of Cups and the Lovers. They were completely out of place with the rest of the reading, so I asked if he was in a relationship with someone he had known previously and if there was a choice pending concerning this relationship. He seemed surprised that this came out in the reading, and reported that he had recently gone back into a relationship which he considered to be serious, but there were aspects he wasn't dealing with. He realized that, by not discussing the situation with his partner, it was actually playing on his mind and affecting other areas of his life—including dealing with his business affairs.

You may also find a link with something from the past that explains the client's fears in position 7. These two cards usually tie together somehow.

Cards 5 and 9—Crowning thoughts and hopes

Similarly, look for the link between these two cards. Are they in conflict? If so, which card will "win"? Remember that the major arcana cards exert a stronger influence, so are more likely to be expressed. Hopefully, you will find harmony between them but obviously that won't always be the case.

If the cards are from the same arcana but show opposing energy, it usually represents conflict within the client. This in itself could pose a problem because in order to achieve their objectives, clients need to be clearly focused and believe in themselves for a positive outcome. Do these cards further explain what the client is experiencing with regard to the card in position 7?

It may sound as though I am repeating myself here, but it cannot be emphasized too strongly how the client's attitudes can affect a situation. By helping clients understand what is being experienced, you can help them move forward more productively. Quite often, this may be why they ask the question in the first place—due to their own doubts and confusion. As you probably realize, this is quite common.

Cards 6 and 10—Immediate future and outcome
Somehow there is a link between these two cards, since the immediate future will lead to the eventual outcome. When this doesn't seem openly apparent, please remember that you are dealing with future situations; therefore, the connection will exist at a future date.

The "what-if" scenarios
I hope you will find this list useful, as it covers most of the areas that people have found puzzling in relation to the Celtic Cross.

What if the last card doesn't seem to be connected?
When this happens, don't let it throw you. Imagine—you're laying down the cards and you can already see the reading is flowing together nicely. Then you place the last card and you just think, "What?" Now, before you dismiss the reading

entirely, take a moment to consider all aspects of it and the positions first. I have found that sometimes when the rest of the reading is going so smoothly, it is easy to hastily discount the card out of hand. Take your time, analyze everything properly; just because this card requires more work doesn't mean it's "wrong." All the cards have reasons to be there.

If you have done this thoroughly yet still feel puzzled by this card's appearance, there are two considerations:

- You are looking at an intervening situation that will manifest in the future and become important, in relation to the original question.
- The current energies will bring a totally new situation into play.

This is an opportune time to take the last card for a continuation reading and ask for more information relating to it (which we will cover in a moment).

What about the court cards?

Consider all the positions of the Celtic Cross. If the court card that appears in any of the positions is not the client's, then you are looking at the influence of another person. Don't go into a tailspin over this; just read the cards as they relate to their relevant positioning, exactly as before. For example:

In the first position: The person represented by the court card is somehow connected to the present situation, or the reason for the question.

In the second: This person has an influence on the situation.

In the third: This person has somehow played a part in the background or history of the question.

In the fourth: This person's involvement has recently passed or is now passing.

In the fifth: Why is this person important in the client's mind?

In the sixth: The person represented by this card is about to enter the situation and has relevance to the immediate future.

In the seventh: Why does the client have apprehensions about this person? If not presently, he or she may feel that way in the future, rightly or wrongly.

In the eighth: The person represented by this card has or will have strong views about the situation.

In the ninth: The client is experiencing (or will experience) positive feelings about this person in relation to the question.

In the tenth: This person is somehow responsible for or relevant to the outcome to the client's question. He or she is an important link.

What if none of the cards seems related to the question?

If your client has asked a question about business and all the cards appear to relate to a relationship—or vice versa—first ask the client if there is a reason these cards should appear or if they relate to a totally separate situation. Your client doesn't have to furnish you with all the details if it is a matter unrelated to their original question. However, advise clients that the cards are trying to inform them of a situation which they need to be aware of at this time. You can then come back to the original question once this message has been relayed to the client. Inform the client that this must be important or else it would not have intervened. Should this be ignored, you will probably find that the cards will be persistent on this matter until they are heard!

This is not an unusual situation. Similarly, if you find most, or even all, of the cards are from the major arcana, then again the Tarot is trying to convey a message of importance, regardless of what the original question was.

What if all the cards seem jumbled up and disconnected?

When this happens, you will usually find that the client has a great deal going on in his or her life presently, so you are actually looking at a number of differing issues happening at the same time. I have a few clients whose cards are almost always this way, but it is simply a reflection of their lives— manically busy. This said, more than a few were Queen of Wand types! Usually you will find that, although there are differing themes running, they still link— like two or more separate stories running simultaneously. With patience and some work, you will see the links.

There is a separate reading that follows, which I call the Life Spread, and I open all my readings with it; this tends to help decipher just what is going on around the client. Then, if necessary, I use the Celtic Cross if there are important questions left unanswered (which is unusual), if more information is needed, or if timing is particularly important to the circumstances.

What if I need more information?

Sometimes the cards will illuminate a situation, or person, about which you feel you need more information. In this case, you take this card and make it the start of a new spread with all the emphasis being upon opening up the situations around it, or how it continues into the future. You may wish to use another Celtic Cross spread or, alternatively, another spread that you feel would be more helpful. However, you must remember to read the positions in the new spread in the context of the fact that you are either exploring more information around that card or, if you are continuing, that you are traveling further into the future.

There are pros and cons in doing this and, if you haven't been using Tarot for very long, I would be reluctant to continue the reading more than once. Even an experienced Tarot reader can become tied up in knots with this technique! Let me explain. Usually the cards reveal all the information required at the present time—if anything else were of further importance, then it would have been revealed. What you have been given is sufficient knowledge for the moment.

In using this technique, it is tempting to just keep going—but at what point do you stop? I have tested this method many times over the years, together with a good friend, and we have discovered that often the cards will just take us around in circles, so we're no wiser than when we first started. The Tarot has a way of letting you know when enough is enough!

Timing with the Celtic Cross

Finding a system of timing that really worked was the one area that seemed to evade me. I tried different methods, painstakingly recording them, until finally I came across this one. I regret I cannot take credit for this method; it came from Eileen Connolly's *Tarot: A New Handbook for the Apprentice, Classic Edition*[1], and my sincere thanks silently went out to her when I finally heard of it. I don't use all her system, as I have found that by narrowing the dates down to specific days, I achieved less reliable results, but the format I use it in has worked extremely well and has proved to be sufficient.

Although I have tried to use this timing format in other spreads, I have found that it has only held true with the Celtic Cross. At least that is my own experience to date. You may wish to experiment with it, and you may find you achieve good results with other spreads, but I suggest you test it upon yourself first, recording your results in the usual way.

---

1. Connolly, Eileen. *Tarot: A New Handbook for the Apprentice, Classic Edition.* (Franklin Lakes, NJ: New Page Books, 1979).

There is some difference of opinion concerning which suits correspond to which season; however, I have stayed true to the recommended format and I can only report it has worked beautifully for me.

The Aces represent:

- Ace of Cups—from the beginning of March
- Ace of Wands—from the beginning of June
- Ace of Swords—from the beginning of September
- Ace of Pentacles—from the beginning of December
- To be recognized as a "timing card," the ace must appear in positions 5, 6, 7, 8, or 9, since the previous cards are "background" cards.
- If more than one ace appears in these positions, you always work with the first ace.
- The number of the card in position 10 provides the number of weeks from the beginning of the appropriate month in relation to the ace.

For example, the Empress (card number 3) is in position 10; the Ace of Pentacles appears in position 6. This would give a timing of three weeks from the beginning of December, so the seven days of that particular week would be relevant.

- If the last card is unnumbered (the Fool, or a court card), simply work backward from the tenth card until you find the first numbered card.
- All cards are broken down to a single digit, so 10 becomes 1 + 0 = 1; 12 becomes 1 + 2 = 3, and so on.
- Always read the ace with its original interpretation first.

I'm sure you have already calculated that this reduces your timing to four lots of nine weeks, which would only give thirty-six weeks in the year. However, it is always important with timing to allow some leeway, as frequently timing depends on varying circumstances, a number of which may be outside the client's control. Even when it relies upon the client, his or her attitude can alter the timing of the event.

The aces in each of the positions simply correspond to what that position relates to. So a timing card in position 6 has far more likelihood of manifesting at this time than an ace in positions 5, 7, or 9, which are more reliant upon the client's attitude, particularly position 7 (representing his or her fears). In position 8, the timing is in some way reliant upon others' actions, either collectively for general questions or, if the question relates to a named person, then that particular person's actions will be relevant.

Sometimes you will find that no matter how much you ask, no timing cards will appear, in which case don't try to force the issue. There are various reasons for this: perhaps events haven't yet unfolded sufficiently for the timing to be set in motion or the universe understands that it actually wouldn't be to the client's benefit to have the information at this time. The Tarot works in mysterious ways and it's best to trust the cards. Perhaps if the client knew the timing, he or she would behave differently, preventing the results altogether. For whatever reason, I find it is best to follow the Tarot's lead. You may want to try a second time, but if the timing still doesn't appear, then I would leave it alone.

I have come across methods in which the reader works back through the deck until he or she finds an ace; however, I feel this is a forced issue and so it's not a format that I follow.

The Life Spread and the Anchor

These two spreads, used simultaneously, are the ones I prefer to use now in my readings. They were developed over a number of years, after feeling frustrated with various limitations I discovered when doing readings, particularly for others. Different spreads have different uses; all have their own place, dependent upon the circumstances.

Spreads with "fixed" positions and interpretations are excellent when you need to pin a situation down and zoom in on something. However, you will find that sometimes this is too limiting and you need to allow more freedom of expression from the cards, as in the "non-fixed" Life Spread.

At first it may seem daunting—twenty-one cards with no particular fixed aspect. But you will find with experience and practice that the Life Spread (combined with the Anchor) can actually answer virtually every question relevant to the client at that particular time in his or her life. To further reassure you, I have known some students who reported that they found this spread easier to work with than the Celtic Cross, even though they were just beginners.

The Life Spread gives a complete overview of all present events that are pertinent and the potential future in each area of the client's life. What I have found is that many people who come with a particular question are experiencing tunnel vision and "can't see the forest for the trees" situations. For the reader, it's important that you have an overall picture, in order for you to provide accurate guidance for your clients—since other aspects of their life will still have a bearing on the question they're asking. It also prevents the situation we covered earlier, in which you ask a question of the cards and they refer to an entirely different situation—because the Tarot understands which situations have relevance and are important for the client to know at this time.

Alongside the Life Spread, I use the Anchor, for which you need a separate deck made up of only the twenty-two major arcana cards. It is so named because the Anchor stays in place throughout the entire reading, regardless of whether the Life Spread is collected and a different spread (such as the Celtic Cross) is put down. The Anchor stays in place and is referred to throughout the readings. We shall cover these spreads together, since they work in conjunction.

- Due to the nature of these spreads, a question is not required.
- Firstly, take your separate deck of the twenty-two major arcana cards; shuffle, cut, and collect in the usual way.
- Take your other deck of seventy-eight cards; shuffle, cut, and collect in the usual way.
- From your first deck shuffled (the twenty-two majors) lay out the Anchor to the right of your cloth.

- Then take your main deck of seventy-eight cards and lay them out alongside, as shown for the Life Spread.
- Take your time and lay the cards into position purposefully. This will allow you to absorb the energies of the cards as you become aware of them.

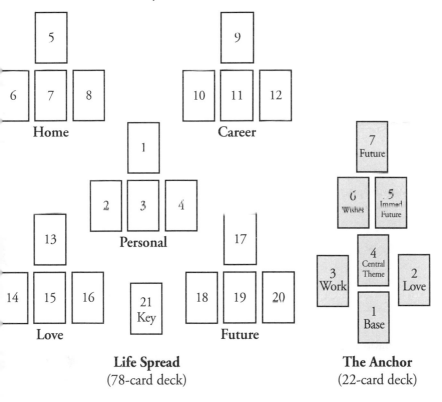

Life Spread
(78-card deck)

The Anchor
(22-card deck)

Life Spread positions

Card positions 1, 2, 3, and 4—The client

How the client feels (or will feel) and what is most important, from the client's perspective. These cards generally provide an overview of what the client is personally experiencing in relation to all aspects of his or her life. You may find that one particular theme stands out here or, alternatively, it can be multi-themed. How do these cards relate to card number 1 in the Anchor?

Card positions #5, 6, 7, and 8—Home

Shows events that impact or are important to the client's home life.

Card positions #9, 10, 11, and 12—Work

Relevant to the client's business or working life.

Card positions #13, 14, 15, and 16—Love and relationships

Shows those influences and events surrounding the client's love life and personal relationships.

Card positions #17, 18, 19, and 20—Future

Shows future events that will unfold. These can be linked to any (or sometimes all) of the other areas.

Card position #21—Key card

The last card is known as the key card and it provides information or advice about what is most important for the client to know at this time. It can either reflect the overall influence regarding his or her current situation or it can show the future sphere of influence that will be prominent.

Look to see how this card interacts with the rest of the reading. Is the card positive? Does it indicate if challenges will be met even if the reading is positive? Does it show delays, blocks, or underhandedness around the client? In that case, the client needs strength, patience, or better awareness to deal with matters.

The key card shows influences the client needs to be aware of and often provides helpful advice or clarification.

Card positions #1, 5, 9, 13, and 17—Influence

These cards all show an important factor at work in relation to the relevant areas—this can be the client's state of mind, another person who is or will be influential, or events that are most pertinent. It can show either present or future influences, but other cards present, and your client, will clarify.

The Anchor

Card position #1—Basis or foundation

Always start your entire reading with this card, as this is the client's present experience.

Card position #2—Love

Connects to cards 13, 14, 15, and 16 from the Life Spread.

Card position #3—Work

Connects to cards 9, 10, 11 and 12 from the Life Spread.

Cards 2 and 3 from the Anchor show what the client is presently experiencing in these areas of his or her life, but may also show what is about to come into being. If the cards reflect the present, then look to cards 5 and 7 for more information regarding the future.

Card position #4—Central position

Shows the client's central position, in connection to all other areas of his or her life. This card can be linked to any of the other areas in the Life Spread, as it shows how he or she will react, so it is an important point of reference. Depending upon circumstances, the client may already be experiencing the effects of this card.

Card position #5—Immediate future

This card will show what is about to come into being and how events will unfold. Look to your main reading to see if there is a particular link, or if it is more generic, covering more than one area.

Card position #6—Wishes

This is an important card because it shows what the client would like to happen. Is the energy of the card working for or against the events that are coming in? I have found Death or the Tower card in this position when clients feel a pressing need to move forward in their life but felt "stuck" for some time, so they have really desired change. It is a very interesting and revealing card.

Card positions #7—Future

The influence of this card ties in with all the cards that relate to future situations, but it represents the overall effect of where the client is heading. Look for the connection with cards 17, 18, 19, and 20 from the Life Spread.

Points to note:

Since we are following a reading with a "non-fixed" aspect, the following information should help clarify how to read the spreads.

How the "non-fixed" spreads differ and rules that apply

In a "fixed" aspect spread, such as the Celtic Cross, all of the positions have a specific interpretation. For example: position 1—present; position 2—influence; position 3—past issues; position 4—immediate past.

However, by allowing the cards freedom of expression, as in a non-fixed spread, they will reveal the course of events as they are appropriate for each client individually, so this will provide various combinations:

- Referring to each area (group of four), you may find that three cards deal with the past and present of a situation, with the fourth showing what is coming in.
- Alternatively, card 2 may show an existing situation, with cards 3 and 4 showing how events will progress, and card 1 showing what the main focus will be.

The only rule here is that the cards are always read in progression 2—3—4; that is, you can't go "back over" yourself. The energy is always moving from left to right, past or present to future.

For example, if card 2 were a present card and card 3 shows future events, then card 4 could never be a past aspect. The cards may show past—present—future, present—present—future, or present—future—future, and occasionally they may all show future events, but they can never go into reverse. Just think of time, as it is in true fashion, always forward-moving.

The key cards

The card at the top of each grouping is a key card, or consolidation. This means that it will inform you of either:

- What is an important influence now.

or

- What will be of importance in the future.

So cards 1, 5, 9, 13, and 17 are relevant to each area as a key card and should tie the other three cards together, within their own particular grouping of four.

Impact on area groupings

You will find that if one area of a client's life holds particular significance, it will literally spill over into the other areas. Don't feel concerned if, for instance, the client's work cards seem to continue or repeat themselves in the home or relationship areas. This in itself is giving you vital information, so don't feel that because the area says "Home" that you have to make the cards fit, when it is evident they don't. However, the title of the area is still important.

Some examples of this could be:

- The client's life is not balanced and he or she is prone to focusing too much on work, such as someone who has workaholic tendencies.
- Work takes precedence at this time and the results affect other areas of the client's life (promotion or fear of layoffs, for instance), so this is the client's main focus.
- The client works or runs a business from home or has a family business.
- He or she may be considering starting a business from home or getting a loan against the family home to do so.
- It makes sense to consider that a man facing bankruptcy would be overwhelmed with financial thoughts, and such a situation would obviously impact everything else in his life.
- Similarly, people about to get married (or divorced) probably show relationship cards seeping into other areas of their life.
- Love cards found in the work area are quite commonplace, often signaling a relationship that starts with someone the client meets at (or who is somehow connected to) the workplace.

These are just some examples of how differing circumstances can affect other areas in a client's life. Take your time and let the Tarot speak to you. Allow the cards to give you the information they want to tell, without feeling the need to stereo-type them into boxes.

It is important not to race ahead or jump to conclusions; there is still a reason the spread is divided into topic areas. If the complete reading were entirely non-fixed, there would be no structure at all, just twenty-one cards drawn and laid in succession.

You need to explore the possibilities of each area. A work offer in the love area could be that the client's partner is suggesting they go into business together, or perhaps the partner provides a contact for a new job offer. Do you see how the combinations can work? So the title of the grouping area does still hold relevance.

Connection to the Anchor Spread

Always refer back to the Anchor—consider it your "clarification reading," as it always holds precedence because the cards are majors. Another interesting feature here is that if any of the major arcana cards are repeated—that is, they show up in both spreads—they hold a very strong significance to the reading.

As an example, let's assume that in the love area of the Life Spread, you have a king that is established to be the partner, the Three of Swords (quarrels) and the Five of Wands (conflicts). The key card shows the Two of Swords (stalemate) but in the Anchor you see Temperance in the love area. Although we can see that the couple is experiencing problems and, due to the progression, we can see that as things stand the future potential doesn't show resolution, the Temperance card in the Anchor provides guidance and understanding of how the situation can be resolved. By understanding this, the client can break the deadlock that exists, with the hope of achieving harmony and cooperation in her relationship.

Usually other cards can also strengthen this, in the future positions, but it depends on how much of a priority the situation is, in relation to other areas of the client's life at this time. So the cards from the Anchor can either strengthen existing information in the Life Spread, or can elaborate and provide further information.

This may all sound very complicated, but I assure you, it is actually easier in practice than it is in theory! These combined spreads are extremely useful in pulling out all sorts of information that will be useful to the client, which you would otherwise be unaware of with a different type of spread.

There is no need for clients to tell you everything before you begin; in fact, you don't want them to, because the cards will reveal all you need to know. However, explain to clients that you will need to ask questions for clarification, but again, you only need the relevant information from their answer—not a complete history or their life story (because you don't want to be influenced by their perspective, or have your judgment colored at this stage). Furthermore, you may find yourself in the position where clients tell you everything; then when you read the cards it sounds as if you're just repeating their words back to them.

Please don't misunderstand me—a reading should always be a two-way exchange. It is the client's reading and for his or her benefit, not yours. You're not there to impress or overwhelm them with startling facts! With this reading, you will need to establish which events are presently around the client in order to follow the progression, so it must be handled with sensitivity. You will find that this makes clients feel very much at ease with you, as you will provide information you otherwise couldn't possibly know, and it will help them have confidence in you as you exchange information throughout the reading.

These two readings combined should provide everything clients need to know, but they can also ask you questions once you have finished the reading. Nine times out of ten, the answer you need will be contained within this layout, without the necessity of producing another spread. It's a really good workhorse! So persevere with it because once you've grasped it, you'll probably find it becomes the main reading you use. As always, use this on yourself first, record the results and your interpretations, then leave a blank page so you can come back later and record events as they actually happened.

Timing for the Life Spread

You should find that events from this spread start to unfold for the client almost immediately. They usually show within three to six months. I have known situations in which other events within the reading have sometimes come to pass later, but it very rarely stretches beyond twelve months.

I don't use the acc timing system for this spread—mainly due to the non-fixed aspect but, in all readings, there are usually other cards that show acceleration in affairs, or delays, or the need for patience, which tend to give some indication of how quickly events will unfold.

The Final Touches

Part Five

Card Associations

Probably more than any other, the Life Spread requires sensitivity to the influences of the cards upon one another. Please remember that with this spread you are always reading a progression of events, the three cards taken one following another in the order they appear from left to right.

With three cards, it is easier to see when one card appears "hemmed in," such as a negative card sandwiched between two positives—or even a card that appears entirely detached from the others. The major arcana cards hold the most influence, but their results may be delayed, restricted, or changed by other cards.

In this instance, we can see deceit is at work. Although the Lovers is central here, the card that follows shows disappointment and regret. The other two cards hamper the positive influence of the Lovers.

However, the cards' meanings alone show you what is to be expected from this outcome. Even if the Lovers were exchanged for the Sun (one of the most positive cards), it would still indicate that, although the situation may show promise, or some respite, it could finally end in disappointment.

However, if the cards were placed like this:

As a progression, you would be looking at quite a different interpretation.

Always look to the surrounding cards to see how the energies merge. Are they in harmony with one another? If there are opposing energies, what does the final card show? Is a positive card "suffocated" by the negative cards around it? Likewise, a negative card surrounded by positive cards can show that the outcome may not be easily achieved—or the situation may not be as perfect as the client would like—but it should not rule out a positive outcome.

Similarly, remember the progression of the suits—what numbers from the suit you are dealing with. The Three of Swords may show quarreling, for example, but its effect is not nearly so bad as, for instance, the Ten of Swords. The Nine of Swords among positive cards can show the client worrying unnecessarily, but together with, say, the Ten of Swords or the Tower, that worry might be justified.

Always read the cards individually, for they each have their own interpretation, but remember that the meanings are influenced and/or altered by the cards that appear alongside.

Sample from the Life Spread

Here is an interesting combination that actually appeared for a client in the future area of his Life Spread:

The client's work area showed an element of deceit and underhandedness at play: the Five of Swords with the King of Pentacles, the Ace of Pentacles, and the Tower. This seemed to indicate either an accountant or bank manager, along with important documents (business financial accounts). This didn't look good with the Tower sitting on the end, showing the unexpected ending of a situation the client believed in.

The combination of cards in the future area (as pictured above) was a curious mix, for they appeared contradictory or jumbled. I felt as if I wanted to rearrange them, so they made more sense to me. However, by staying true to what the cards said, it showed a situation concerning a large amount of money that might also impact the client's home (the Ten of Pentacles) but the client receiving what was rightfully his (the Six of Pentacles) appeared to be affected by someone who didn't seem to want to share, perhaps someone quite "money minded" but overly careful spending it (the Four of Pentacles). I was diplomatic with the interpretation, with a warning of the potential for financial loss (the Five of Pentacles).

Based on the description from the Four of Pentacles, the client said that person sounded like his business partner. Following the reading, he looked into matters and discovered that, without his knowledge, his partner had attended meetings with accountants and advisors, going over the company accounts, with a view to closing the business. My client was dependent on the business, so this would leave him with no income, whereas his partner had other financial means. Some legalities of the situation also showed up, but suffice it to say there was enough information for him to act upon. Considering the cards given in the work area, these cards were quite accurate to the situation that was brewing, but of which the client had no previous knowledge. So you see, it gives an indication of just how literal the cards can be at times.

So although the interpretation sounded a little odd to me, it made perfect sense to the client. Obviously, the reading raised questions about his future and whether he would want to remain in business with this individual. Fortunately, the

Anchor showed good things ahead for him, but the insight from the Life Spread allowed him to make forward-looking plans, instead of being dropped in the proverbial "you know what" by his business partner, which would have left my client in more than an inconvenient position.

The cards you can't relate to

You will find, after a period of time, that there may be certain cards that you just don't seem to connect to—or that you hate when they appear. We all have "blank" cards. I used to dread the Fives more than any others—I'd rather have had the Tower than a Five! At this point, some self-analysis is required.

Draw the cards that you feel are "blank" to you out of the deck. Also do this with the cards that you dislike or feel a strong reaction to. Then take each card in turn and ask yourself the following questions:

- Is there a situation that you are avoiding in your life that connects with these interpretations?
- Have you had a particularly bad past experience in your life that you're reminded of whenever you see this card?

It is important to identify your internal fears of these cards. Mine were the Five of Swords and Five of Cups, a reflection of some painful experiences. I realized that whenever these cards appeared, it immediately invoked old "ghosts," because I related them only to that situation. But the Five of Cups can also mean feelings of regret (not always betrayal or loss) and the Five of Swords can be a warning that you're not fully aware of another's agenda—not always full-blown deceit. So whichever cards may be troublesome for you, look at them more closely, understand what they are teaching you, then put these cards back into perspective. Your view needs to be balanced and uncolored, or else how can you help your client, or even yourself in your own readings?

Now this may seem like a contradiction, after telling you to record your personal experiences that remind you of each card in order to get a good understanding of the card's interpretation. However, it's interesting, when you read all the original interpretations you've recorded, to notice how you may have focused on only one part of them. Insightful, isn't it? If you go back now and look over your original interpretations and the record of your personal experiences, they will tell you much of your own inner feelings. This being the case, take the time now to add other experiences that relate to the other meanings of this card—the areas that your subconscious initially ignored.

It is a very useful exercise for self-examination, recognizing our own fears and dealing with them, because we don't want to project these onto our clients.

About the "awkward" cards

As previously discussed, all the cards have their own relevance but are influenced by the surrounding cards. All of life is about balance. The entire lesson throughout the major arcana is about blending and combining opposites in order to attain the perfection that we seek in our lives (shown in the culmination of the World). It is a rare individual who achieves this without some struggles or adversity along the way.

As a Tarot reader, it is important to treat all your clients' readings with sensitivity. Recognize that we all deal with situations differently; what is traumatic to me may be less so to you, or to another. The so-called "negative" cards all have their place in our lives, but what makes the difference, between one individual and another, is how we deal with the situation.

I have already covered how the Devil can also have a positive aspect and, by and large, its negative influence is self-enslavement, whereby the person can be free of the situation by changing his or her own actions, or taking action.

The Tower—although its effects may be uncomfortable to deal with—always follows events that are built on false beliefs. That may be of little comfort to clients at the time the situation starts to fall apart, but the Tower will release them from a false situation of which they've been ignorant. Therefore, it will allow them the opportunity to build a better life for the future, similar to the client who had the Tower in his work area and the situation with his work partner.

The Death card shows major changes and we have covered how this is not always negative. However, nobody really likes change; it's uncomfortable. Yet most of us have encountered a number of major changes on our journey through life already. Given the choice, at the time, we probably wouldn't have accepted them readily—after all, who wants a relationship breakup, a job loss, a deal that goes wrong, or a move to another area when we thought we were happy where we were? Yet it is amazing how often these major changes lead to new opportunities that we never would have encountered otherwise. New and valuable friends, partners, or lifestyle changes never would have entered our lives without that major change that altered our direction.

Let us not forget that someone getting married is also facing a major change in his or her life, so the interpretation, as we can see, can also have a positive side. As with the people who have Death or the Tower in the area of desires—as they are most wanting change to occur in their lives—it doesn't always mean there is a negative impact, or even that the client will view it to be one.

It is fear of the unknown that usually holds us back. Therefore, as a Tarot reader, you have the opportunity to provide guidance and hope for the future.

Putting it into perspective

I have met many people who have been unnecessarily worried sick by irresponsible readers. I usually ask if they can recount the cards that caused the problem, or what was said, and I have spent a great deal of time reassuring, counseling, and sometimes doing new readings for people, as a result of someone else's thoughtlessness.

For example:

- The woman in tears because she's been told she's going to get divorced.
- The client being told she or her partner are going to have or are having an affair.
- Someone being told of a loved one's death.
- Clients being told they're going to lose their home/ job/income/lover/child.

What will your friends or clients say when they leave your reading? What impact have you had on their life? Did you help them, or give them more to worry about? I'm not suggesting you lie to people and make all your readings falsely glowing if they're not, but your main focus with every client should be to try and help him or her.

Help clients realize that they ultimately have control over their destiny. If they don't like the way the future's heading, what action can they take to bring about a better outcome? What do they need to face realistically to deal with change?

The future is not written in stone, but invariably I have found that the reader has given a wrong interpretation—

sometimes this has been caused by merely one card. This is why earlier I wrote, "One card does not a reading make." Typical examples of misinterpretations include the Three of Swords read as divorce and the Lovers read as an affair; I'm sure I don't even need to cover the rest for you. A number of the people I refer to have become friends or regular clients of mine, having come to see me following their shock reading, and I can honestly report that, in each case, what these people were told by the other reader never came to pass.

In one case, a female client was told she would get divorced. She had a happy marriage, no sign of any problems, and had gone for a general reading. It transpired that the Three of Swords appeared on its own, with no supporting cards such as Death, the Tower or the Ten of Swords. If the reader had bothered to ask, she would have discovered that, at the time, the woman's husband was working away from home and they missed each other dreadfully. They are still happily married today.

As I'm sure you can appreciate, it's a subject you can get quite passionate about when you witness the damage that these so-called readers can cause, both to the person they're reading for and also to the reputation of those readers who do conduct themselves professionally, ethically, and thoughtfully. I hope you understand now why I have tried to impress upon you the importance of reading for yourself first, verifying your interpretations in your diary, and finally, treating other people's lives with great sensitivity.

About illness

You may have noticed that I haven't covered anything regarding illness. This is a tricky subject. I have heard of instances in which readers have systems to tie in specific illnesses to particular cards, but I have to say this has never held true for me. At least that was my experience, and I was quite interested to investigate this, since I'm also a healer. For the most part, you will find that the cards show recovery and healing. Once more I must reiterate that a person's state of mind can have a great effect upon his or her health.

However, what I have discovered is that often, when a serious health problem develops for a client, the Tarot reader or psychic usually didn't detect it. Why is that? In my own view, and from discussions with some excellent psychics I know, it seems that it would not have been in that person's best interest to know—so the psychic never received the information to pass on. Vedic astrologers, in a very accurate science, would tell you a similar story regarding the potential time that a person may leave his or her earthly body, based on the birth chart. It is an area of spirituality that lends itself to a great deal of discussion, for those interested in such matters.

Please forgive me if I relate some personal instances here, but I only share them with you in the hope that they will help you to understand. I once had a fairly simple accident, but sustained awful injuries that resulted in me being laid up for over a year. It was painful! I'd been to see a really wonderful medium not long before, but she never told me about this. Later, when I asked her why she hadn't told me, she informed me that she hadn't been given the information. When we discussed the spiritual aspects of this, it made a great deal of sense. Imagine if I had known—could I have avoided it? I would never have left the house! Now I realize it was one of my most important learning experiences, and shortly after this people started seeking healing from me. But, given the choice, I would never have wanted the accident.

Sometimes the mysterious ways of the universe are best left unknown. Some things are part of our destiny that we can't avoid, but are for our greater good, or hold important lessons for the loved ones whose lives we touch.

My father was one of the kindest people you could ever wish to meet, so caring for him and seeing him suffer in his final years with an awful condition such as Alzheimer's seemed very unjust. We cared for him in our home, along with my mother, and this involved my two teenage children, in whose lives he had always played a major part. It was difficult for all of us and it has taken quite some time for me to come to terms with it, and to start to see the spiritual perspective. But did my Tarot tell me? No. Before he died, was it in my cards? Nothing. I could feel his energy fading but I never was given a time or date, and when the phone call came it was unexpected. Would I have benefited from knowing? I hardly think so.

It is important for you to realize that you can only give the client the information that the Tarot provides you. Using intuition to read the cards is one thing; heading off on your own clairvoyant tangent is quite another. There are some psychics who work exclusively with health issues and have the gift to actually see what is wrong with a person, picking up undiagnosed illnesses or discussing past health problems they couldn't possibly be aware of—but that is an entirely different type of work than Tarot readings.

If it were in our best interests to arrive on this planet with our life clearly laid out before us, then we'd all arrive with a book of detailed instructions and every event clearly defined. But our life is made up of our personal experiences, our journey through our lessons—our own soul growth and our purpose for being here. Our life experiences test and shape us; they offer us choices as to how we react to them, grow through them, learn from them.

As a reader you are like the signpost that guides the way; a beacon of light, to help a confused soul find its way through its moment of darkness and find its way home through the fog. We're not the harbingers of doom. Consider your role carefully, for people tend to consult Tarot readers when they feel they have momentarily lost their direction, when they're confused or need a glimmer of hope. And I believe there's hope for everyone. Never underestimate the power of belief.

From your readings, you will find that the cards show times of stress or times when the client feels overburdened, and if unchecked this can lead to illness. Obviously, indications such as the Four of Swords followed by the Nine or Ten of Swords are different than if the Nine were followed by the Four, for instance. But please tread oh-so-gently, and don't jump to conclusions. You may see difficult times ahead, yet be frustrated by the lack of further information . . . but in due course you will understand why.

We cannot always control what happens around us, but we can control our reaction to it, and we can help those who come to us for guidance.

Card combinations

Various card combinations tend to indicate specific events. It is always important to look for "backup" or confirmation from other cards, so I have placed these in specific groupings in which meanings overlap or strengthen one another.

The following are some that have held true for me, but the list is not exhaustive, definitive, or set in stone. I only offer it as a tentative guide for you to consider in your readings. Watch for these combinations yourself first, then record the reading in the usual manner and verify your results. With regard to the "negative" cards, please always check the client's position first and use sensitivity when relaying information. A great deal of trouble can be avoided by using a thoughtful, careful approach, as we have covered, and anything you can't help with you're not usually shown.

The cards shown would be in progression in the layout, either appearing side by side, or in very close proximity (so long as other cards don't intervene), with backup cards appearing in the spread to strengthen the interpretation.

It is important to realize that commitment to a relationship and a sense of permanency doesn't always translate to marriage in the traditional sense anymore; this especially applies for same-sex relationships. However, cards that represent legalities (marriage certificate) and official offices, such as the church or registry office, sometimes indicate a traditional marriage.

There are quite a few of these combinations concerning relationships because, as you will discover, questions about relationships tend to be among the most frequently asked questions.

Pregnancy/birth	Ace of Wands and the Empress (side by side)
Christening invitation	Page of Cups—the Empress—the Hierophant and Three of Cups
Wedding invitation	Page of Cups—the Hierophant—the Lovers and Three of Cups

Marriage/commitment	Ace of Pentacles—the Lovers—Ten of Cups or Ace of Cups—the Lovers—Ten of Pentacles
(plus backup)	Justice—Four of Wands—the Hierophant—Three of Cups—the Empress—Temperance—the Sun
Making wedding plans	Two of Cups (or the Lovers)—Four of Wands and Three of Cups
Love proposal	Knight of Cups—Ace of Cups—the Lovers
Commitment proposal	Knight of Cups—Two of Cups—the Lovers (or the Empress)
Serious relationship with future plans being made	Two of Cups—the Sun (side by side)
Happy marriage/family life or permanent relationship	Ten of Cups—the Sun (side by side) or Ten of Pentacles—the Sun
Reconciliation and relationship renewal	Judgement—Two of Cups—Temperance (or the Star) Judgement—Six of Cups—Lovers—Temperance

Buying and selling property, new home	Knight of Wands—Ten of Pentacles—Ace of Pentacles—Justice
Recovery from illness	Four of Swords—Six of Swords—The Star—Judgement—Temperance
Inheritances	Ace of Pentacles—Justice—Six of Pentacles—Ten of Pentacles—King of Swords—sometimes Nine of Pentacles
New job	Ace of Wands—Eight of Pentacles
Promotion at work with financial increase	Six of Wands—Six of Pentacles
Situation from the past brought back	Judgement—Knight of Pentacles—Six of Cups—Eight of Wands

Relationship ending	Three of Swords—the Lovers—Ten of Swords—Death
(other cards confirm)	The Tower—Five of Cups—Eight of Cups The Two, or Ten of Cups can show instead of the Lovers but would need to be "sandwiched" in the same way
Deception around client	Five of Swords—the Moon—Seven of Swords—the Devil—Page of Swords—Five of Cups
Stress cards (the more that appear, the greater the effect)	Seven of Wands—Ten of Wands—Eight of Swords—Nine of Swords—Five of Pentacles—Knight of Swords—the Devil—the Moon—Death—the Tower

STEP 22

Living with Tarot

During your studies, the Tarot has probably become an integral part of your life and, I hope, an enjoyable one. Throughout this book, I have constantly made reference to using the cards for yourself and doing self-readings, as this is an important part of your learning development. In so doing, I just want to ensure that we are clear about something quite important.

While I know most Tarot readers do consult their own cards, they don't live their life by them—as such, I mean they're not overly dependent on them. In the early days, you may find you consult the Tarot about almost everything, but as you gain experience, this should fade to a more realistic approach. For instance, I don't consult the Tarot every morning to see what the day will bring, and neither do I consult the cards for minor issues that I am quite capable of thinking through for myself. It is important to develop a healthy relationship with the cards in order to live harmoniously with them.

The Tarot is not a crutch. However, for a regular overview, or when you need guidance about an important issue, or perhaps to steer through a complex situation, they are invaluable. It really is a matter of common sense; the Tarot can assist you on your path, but should not take over or dictate it. If you find you are asking your cards about anything and everything before making a decision, then you are becoming too reliant on them. There is a difference between needed advice and common sense and I'm sure I don't need to point out the difference, or insult your intelligence by trying to do so.

Reading for others

There are many things to consider once you are ready to read for other people and, before you do so, I hope I can assist in pointing out some pros and cons of such.

Without wishing to dampen your enthusiasm, reading for others can be something of a double-edged sword. On the one hand, it can be immensely rewarding; on the other, it can sometimes be quite frustrating. Thankfully, it tends to be more of the former than the latter, if you set things up correctly to begin with and operate with good ethics.

Firstly, you need to check the laws as they pertain to your locality, as you don't want to find that you're inadvertently operating illegally.

The second thing that will help enormously is to ensure that those who consult you for readings know what to expect—in other words, what is and isn't possible, how long the reading will take, the format it will take, and their involvement in the process—since the reading is a two-way exchange, not a psychic test to see how much you can uncover about them without being told!

This is normally where the question of whether or not you should charge for your readings arises. The difficulty is that if you provide your readings for free (and you're good), you may find you're inundated with requests as word travels. Now, while in the early days this may be quite flattering, there comes a point when what once was an enjoyment feels like a chore. If you're quite happy to continue reading for free, then that's no problem—but if you are the kind of person who will have difficulty in being assertive later (by saying "no," because it isn't convenient) or risk being taken advantage of, then there are a number of things you can do to ensure that this doesn't happen to you.

With your very closest friends, you can offer to read for free, but let them know that if others they know would like to have a reading, you need to charge for your time. My friends were very good, as they always offered to pay for readings anyway; instead, I would tell them that if they were pleased, just let others know about me. This in itself can bring you many referrals, and then neither you nor your friends will feel awkward about the money thing.

You can use your readings as an exchange of energy, or you can exchange favors—some people feel far more comfortable with this, particularly if you don't want the hassle of additional income that then has to be accounted for, considered for taxes, and so on. You can exchange the favor for baby-sitting, gardening, a haircut—you name it. People have also sent me all kinds of gifts I hadn't even anticipated, in thanks for a reading that helped them.

There is nothing wrong with charging for readings; what you are offering people is your time and skill, just as with anything else for which we exchange our money. You don't expect your car to be fixed for free just because the person can do it, do you? To ascertain what you should charge, it really depends on how valuable your time is, how experienced you are, and what constitutes a fair price in your area for your services.

You may also wish to consider whether this is to be a part-time venture or a full-time occupation; there is quite a difference. I will never forget a conversation I had a number of years ago with a professional psychic. She was really good and I was quite surprised to hear that at times she felt quite jaded. She explained that every day she was asked the same kind of questions, and it was immensely frustrating that some people never learned, regardless of the advice she gave. She didn't feel like this all the time, but it was a valuable insight for me.

Do you really want your Tarot readings to feel like a "job"? Only you can answer this. There is a difference between doing something because you enjoy it and doing it because you have to pay the bills. I think once it becomes the latter, there is the danger of losing your passion for it. Now, I am not suggesting that everyone who goes full time does or will feel this way—some people just love it! But now you are looking at a proper business and all that this entails. You need to consider how much income you need to support you and your business expenses, how you would get regular customers, and you would need a professional environment to operate from. If this is from home, can you ensure there will be no crying children, loud televisions, or noisy pets? As with any business, it will take time to develop; it won't be successful overnight. So you see, there is quite a lot to consider.

Reading for minors

I always recommend getting the permission of a parent before reading for youngsters—unfortunately, there can be some misunderstanding surrounding the cards and there are still those who incorrectly associate the Tarot with evil or dark forces. You wouldn't wish to find yourself on the receiving end of such accusations from an upset parent. In addition, teenagers can be very suggestible and so their readings need to be handled even more carefully than those for an adult.

Teenagers experience difficulties in their lives that are just as serious to them as their adult counterparts. Perhaps due to our modern way of life, young people today feel under more pressure and have more stress and problems that affect them in a serious way. One only needs to look at the increase in youth suicide and crime rates. Those I have read for found their readings uplifting and helpful in moving forward more confidently with their lives. This can be a very rewarding experience for you both, but please, tread very gently, as young people tend to be extremely impressionable.

If you have youngsters of your own, then the Tarot provides a wonderful tool. You will be amazed what your teenager will accept and the failings/insecurities/problems he or she will freely admit to based upon what the Tarot has to say (as opposed to "you" having offered it). It is much less confrontational or accusatory and, if you do this correctly, unbiased. Even if you have a good relationship with your children and normally discuss problems openly together, you may still be pleasantly surprised by the extra dimension the Tarot can bring to your relationship. I never force Tarot upon my children and to this day my son has never asked for a reading, but my daughter has, from time to time. It doesn't replace your normal relationship, but it can enhance it. Then don't be surprised if they ask to borrow your book to learn for themselves!

Some final words

Within these twenty-two steps, I have covered everything you should need to read Tarot cards successfully. With practice, experience, and sincerity of purpose the Tarot will reward your efforts—persistence pays.

Your experience with the Tarot is very much a personal journey and, like all spiritual pathways, it is one where you need to find your own "truth." So far, you have been following what I perceive as my truth—by this I mean that after many years of searching, studying, and practice, this is what the Tarot has come to mean to me, and how it works for me.

In the early days, I discovered that it's important to stay with one system until you've really grasped it, rather than merging many different theories, which can be confusing and quite contradictory. But later I found that whenever I changed my interpretations, or opted for other methods, my results suffered, resulting in the system we have shared together in this book. The Tarot has a way of building an affinity with you, a silent understanding of what you're looking for from the cards, so if you start to change things they also become "confused." Allow time for any changes that you may wish to introduce.

However, having followed my system, and once you become proficient in it, you may then wish to strike out on your own, exploring the many possibilities in the world of Tarot. There are many new books and interesting theories being created all the time, all offering differing thoughts and insights. What I will say, though, is to keep using your diary, always test your results and verify them later, then trust your intuition, for by this time it should be well-developed. Then you must do what is right for you, your truth. Of course, you can always consult your Tarot!

Practice, practice, practice—and finally, once you feel happy with your readings and confident with yourself and your Tarot, then that is the time to start offering your newfound skills to provide guidance for your friends.

For now at least, our time together has come to a close. We have reached the crossroads where you take your path and I take mine . . . I hope you have enjoyed our journey together as much as I.

May your path be filled with many blessings and the abundance of all good things.

Love & Light,
Josie

Useful Tools
and Templates

Part Six

These cheat sheets are useful tools. They contain only key words, as they are intended to be used as a memory jogger and not to replace the full descriptions of each card.

Minor Arcana Cheat Sheet

Suit	Wands	Cups
Element	Fire	Water
	Action and initiative, inspiration, career.	Love and emotions, relationships, creativity.
Ace	New venture or way of life. Pregnancy or birth.	New relationship. New start that brings happiness for all at home.
Two	Initial accomplishment. Possible partnership.	Important union. Balance in a relationship, reconciliation.
Three	Completion of first stage of project. Progress.	Happiness and achievement. Wedding/family celebrations.
Four	Stability. Holidays. Marriage plans.	Boredom and discontent.
Five	Conflict, quarrelling, competition.	Feelings of disappointment, letdown or betrayal. Regrets.
Six	Success, achievement, promotions.	Happiness from the past. Old friends, an old love revived.
Seven	Defending position, overcoming obstacles.	Feeling overwhelmed with choices; one must be made. Imagination.
Eight	Fast progress after delays. Travel.	Abandoning a path. Disillusionment, emotionally unfulfilled.
Nine	Perseverence; pull reserves together for final push.	The "wish" card. Emotional and material fulfilment.
Ten	Feeling overburdened, weary. Determination required.	Committed and contented love. Marriage. Happy home life.
Page	Good news (work related). Active, cheerful child.	Happy news (emotional nature). Sensitive, creative child.
Knight	Change of home or long journey. Energetic young man.	Love proposals. Romantic, idealistic young man.
Queen	Warm, cheerful, woman, always very busy.	Kind, thoughtful, sensitive woman with caring nature.
King	Entrepreneurial, dynamic man who can be rash.	Warm, thoughtful man, in the caring or creative professions.

Minor Arcana Cheat Sheet

Suit	Swords	Pentacles
Element	Air	Earth
	Intellect, analytical thought, challenges and animosity.	Material aspects of life, finance, property, etc.
Ace	Triumph over adversity. Inner strength and mental clarity.	Start of successful venture. Important document. Gift.
Two	Stalemate.	Maintaining balance with more than one area of life.
Three	Quarrelling. Misery through separation.	Success through effort. Gains and recognition
Four	Rest and recovery following strain.	Overly cautious, fear of loss. Material focus (or miserly).
Five	Deceit, hidden agenda, unfair dealings.	Temporary hardship. Guard against loss.
Six	Harmony after strain. Long journey over water.	Successful gains. Sharing. Gift.
Seven	Diplomacy, not aggression. Situation not going as anticipated.	Work and patience rewarded. Good news financially.
Eight	Feeling restricted by fear. Being withdrawn.	New job, moneymaking venture from existing talent.
Nine	Sense of anxiety and despair. Feelings of oppression.	Financial success and material security.
Ten	Disappointment. End of cycle. Failed plans.	Financial and family stability. Property. Inheritance.
Page	Delayed/disappointing news. Minor problems with a child	Good news (financial). Academic, methodical child.
Knight	Swift movement, chaotic. Quick minded, serious young man.	Eventual positive outcome. Reliable young man.
Queen	Perceptive lady, efficient, no-nonsense type.	Woman of worth, capable and practical.
King	Man in uniform, connected to law, government, etc.	Successful man who works with finance/figures.

Major Arcana Cheat Sheet

Number	Title	Meaning
0	The Fool	Unexpected opportunity, major choice.
I	The Magician	You have the ability you need to succeed. Mastery.
II	The High Priestess	Intuition, secrets to be revealed, unexplored potential.
III	The Empress	Nurturing to full potential, marriage, motherhood.
IV	The Emperor	Ambition, authority, financial stability, achievement.
V	The Hierophant	Traditional values, a wise person provides guidance.
VI	The Lovers	Love relationship, perhaps love choices.
VII	The Chariot	Triumph over difficulties, strength of will needed.
VIII	Strength	Gentleness with inner strength and courage.
IX	The Hermit	Withdrawal for contemplation, inner wisdom.
X	The Wheel of Fortune	Change of fortune, a new cycle commencing, progress.

Major Arcana Cheat Sheet

Number	Title	Meaning
XI	Justice	Fairness, the need for a balanced mind, legal matters.
XII	The Hanged Man	Understanding, different perspective, self-sacrifice.
XIII	Death	Major change, transformation.
XIV	Temperance	Patience, moderation, compromise, balance, healing.
XV	The Devil	Manipulation, overindulgence, self-enslavement.
XVI	The Tower	Destruction of something built upon false beliefs.
XVII	The Star	Hope, healing, optimism, better times ahead.
XVIII	The Moon	Uncertainty, illusion, fluctuating emotions, unseen depth.
XIX	The Sun	Success, happiness, good health, happy marriage.
XX	Judgement	Renewal, revival, reward for past efforts. Karma.
XXI	The World	Triumph and achievement, success and happiness.

The Cross of Truth template

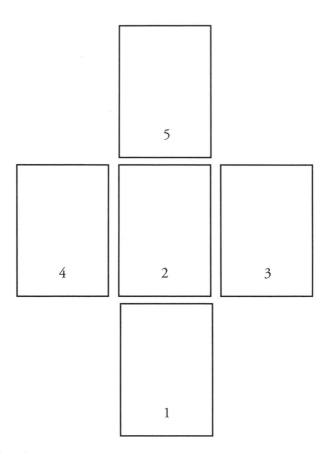

5

4

2

3

1

Question:

The Celtic Cross template

Date:

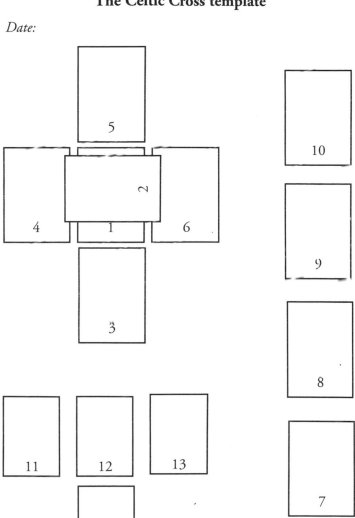

The Life Spread template

Date:

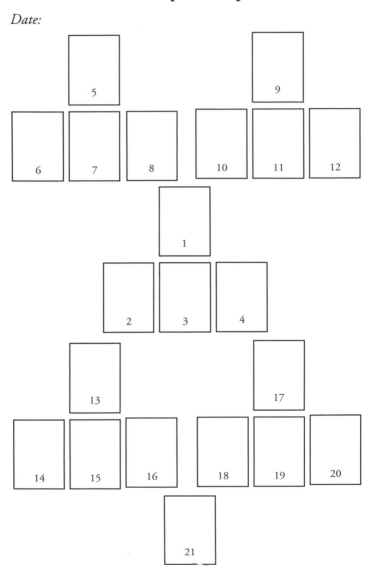

The Anchor template

Date:

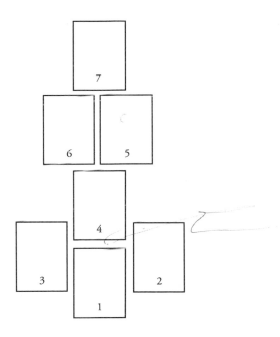